Engaging Your Imagination for Raising Godly Children

How to Create Spiritual Giants

By

Rachael Testa

Engaging Your Imagination for Raising Godly Children

How to Create Spiritual Giants

By

Rachael Testa
2941 Baas Road
Green Lane, Pennsylvania 18054

Engaging Your Imagination for Raising Godly Children
How to Create Spiritual Giants

Copyright © 2024 Rachael Testa

Scripture is taken from the New King James Version®. Copyright © 1982 by Thomas Nelson. Used by permission. All rights reserved. (Unless otherwise noted.)

Scripture quotations marked (NLT) are taken from the New Living Translation®. Copyright © 1996, 2004, 2007, 2013, 2015 by Tyndale House Foundation. Used by permission of Tyndale House Publishers, Inc., Carol Stream, Illinois 60188. All rights reserved.

Any trademarks mentioned are the property of their respective owners.

All rights reserved. This book is protected by the copyright laws of the United States of America. This book may not be copied or reprinted for commercial gain or profit. The use of short quotations or occasional page copying for personal, or group study is permitted and encouraged. Permission will be granted upon request.

Requests for bulk sales discounts, editorial permissions, or other information should be addressed to:

Scroll Publishers
PO Box 5847
Pinehurst, NC 28374 USA

Additional copies available at www.scrollpublishers.com

ISBN 13 TP: 978-1-962808-06-4
ISBN 13 eBook: 978-1-962808-03-3

Cover by Darian Horner (DarianHornerDesign.com)
Image: elements.envato.com FQYQ6AZ

First Edition: June 2024

10 9 8 7 6 5 4 3 2 1 0

Printed in the United States of America

Table of Contents

Acknowledgements i

Foreword iii

Preface v

Chapter 1 The Word of God 1

Chapter 2 Speaking Prayers and the Word of Your Testimony .. 5

Chapter 3 Worship with Your Children 9

Chapter 4 Speak Spirit to Spirit 13

Chapter 5 A Combined Application 29

Chapter 6 The Observer Effect 39

Chapter 7 Inner Healing 53

Chapter 8 Expanding Past Yourself 59

Chapter 9 Hearing God's Voice 65

Chapter 10 Learning to Hear God's Voice 69

Chapter 11 Heavenly Alignment 73

Chapter 12 Realm Angels and the Process 89

Chapter 13 Mastering the Mind 93

Chapter 14 Aligning Your Realms Script 105

Chapter 15 The Ancient of Days.. 109

Chapter 16 A New Master Blueprint.. 113

Chapter 17 Prophetic Acts and More Revelation 117

Chapter 18 Review... 125

Appendix..127

    Opening Prayer..127

    Closing Prayer... 131

    The Names of God..135

    Ministries Mentioned 139

About the Author 141

Description... 143

Acknowledgements

Thank you, God, for unmerited favor. Thank you to my husband Andrew for your trust, support, love, and desire for me to do what brings me joy even when you do not fully understand it. Thank you to my kids for coming on this journey with me and for sharing openly what the Lord and your spirits show you. Thank you to my brothers and sisters in Christ who have encouraged and helped me process though this journey in all the different ways. Thank you to the ministers and ministries who have poured into me so that I could process it through my quantum emotions, spirit, soul, and body, and pour it out onto these pages. Thank you to my quantum emotions, spirit, soul, and body for communicating with each other.

Foreword

I had the blessing of meeting Rachael at Dr. Ron Horner's July 2023 conference in Pinehurst, North Carolina. Soon after I had the pleasure of visiting her via messenger video and with her son Ben. Right away I could tell that Ben was special. Rachael takes her role as a believer and parent seriously. It is also clear to me that we live in a time when revelation and resources are pouring out of Heaven and that Rachael is taking advantage of these resources as she seeks to help Ben be the best "son" he can be.

Having four sons myself I can tell you that the busy things of life can so easily sidetrack us from our key role as a parent which is to help our children embrace their gifts and callings as well as heavenly resources and culture. A part of this is to establish a format by where our children learn to apply those gifts and callings in their everyday life, and this is in a practical and demonstratable way. Guess what? The parent also grows and benefits from the process.

It is my pleasure to recommend the contents of her book as a spiritual parenting guide to help you raise your child as a true son or daughter of the King. It is a very practical read and if put into practice then you should expect tremendous results.

Thank you, Rachael, for not just being a hearer but a doer of the Word.

Dr. Robert Rodich
docrodich.com

Preface

My name is Rachael, and I am a mom raising godly children living in a blended family. I am remarried and have a wonderful husband, Andrew, and twin stepdaughters, Gabby and Bella, who are 14. Ben is my 9-year-old son from my first marriage.

My husband and I are co-parenting with four other parents,[1] us and two others on each side of our children. The Lord is working in our family, but I am restricted in how much I can share regarding my stepdaughters, so I will focus on the journey Ben and I have been taking. God is doing a new thing, and I want to share it with you so you can experience the kind of breakthroughs we have been experiencing in our parenting. Let's pray,

> *Ancient of Days, Father God, Jesus, and Holy Spirit, we invite you into this journey. Thank you for putting the words on these*

---

[1] Our former spouses co-parent with us through joint custody arrangements.

pages that you want received by these readers. Thank you for guiding each of them to this reading and guiding them every step of the way through this journey. They will have peace and confidence in what you are speaking through this. They will apply it well.

Thank you for not allowing them to be diverted or go astray. We open the eyes of our understanding to your wisdom, guidance, knowledge, understanding, strength, Spirit, and the fear of the Lord. We open the eyes of our understanding to your love, joy, peace, patience, kindness, gentleness, goodness, generosity, faithfulness, and self-control. We are quantum beings and call for heavenly alignment for our emotions: spirit, soul, and body.

We request and thank you for heavenly resources to assist us on this journey in Jesus' name.

Parenting is challenging, but do not fear, worry, feel lost, or overwhelmed; God is with you! He gave us his helper, the Holy Spirit, to commune and work with our spirits.

1 Corinthians 2:11

After all, who can really see into a person's heart and know his hidden impulses except for that person's spirit?

God's Spirit knows the thoughts and hearts of the Father and the Son, and our spirit knows the thoughts and hearts of us, our bodies, and souls. That is how God communicates with us; our children are no different. God communicates with them in conjunction with the Holy Spirit and their spirit. So, where do we start in leading our children in the way they should go?

First, be the example. Start now if you are not doing the things you want your children to do. Today is a new day, and there is mercy and grace for when we mess up. Jesus was born of a virgin, was innocent, died on the cross for our sins, defeated death, and hell, and rose again on the third day. He has redeemed us, and now He sits at the Father's right hand and intercedes on our behalf. We are redeemed! We are sons and daughters of the Most High God. We also sit in heavenly places and intercede for the redemption of others, including our children and the world they live in. That is what you are doing when you are praying for your children. Take it seriously. Our children need to be equipped with the Word of God, and understand how to use it, and so do we! When we teach our children, the Lord will often work through them, and in their innocence and response, they will teach us. The Lord will speak to you through what your child says and does. It happened to me!

This will be an amazing journey not just for them but for you, too! Isn't that exciting? I am excited! I bless you in this endeavor! I encourage you to start these steps and then, as you continue your journey, implement them simultaneously. Don't wait years to finish step one before you go to step two.

Chapter 1
The Word of God

Expose your children to the direct, unfiltered Word of God. Find a program that takes you through the Bible in a year and do it with your children every day. It could be in the morning or evening before bed. I love using the dailyaudioBible.com (the DAB). It is important for your kids to hear the Word of God as it is written in the Bible and to get the context. The DAB is a great way to get the word and the context. It provides good, clean commentary and uses multiple translations for perspective.

If you or your kids keep falling asleep while listening, that's great! Use it as a bedtime tool, but that tool is secondary. You must prioritize it, so also listen during the waking hours. Listen twice! When I listen twice, I hear different things but not contradicting things. Sometimes, because of distraction or zoning out, I had to become intentional about that because the enemy and myself, my body and soul, kept coming at me with distractions. Sometimes, the different things popping out at me were because it is the living Word of God.

The DAB is designed so that you can get new insights, and it can speak differently to you each time you listen to it or read it. It is quite an amazing phenomenon, which is fun and encouraging to experience!

Your children may be restless while you are trying to listen or read with them. My 5-year-old would not sit still. In this case, I suggest listening in the car where they are strapped in and have nothing better to do. This worked out well for me. We would listen every time we were in the car until we got through that day's podcast.

Sometimes, Ben would be playing in the back, talking, or singing, sitting as unstill as possible in a car seat, but then he would randomly come up with questions that would let me know that he was listening, paying attention, and absorbing it. Do not use the kid's versions or go through the Bible stories and skip parts of the Bible; it is all important even when we don't think it is. I was amazed at how much detail is in the Bible that was left out in my upbringing because I didn't sit down and read/listen to the Bible for myself. I grew up with it all: Bible verses and the stories, Sunday school, church, clubs like Awana, and youth group.

When I started listening to the DAB in 2019, I started listening on May 15th, where they read about the story of David and Goliath. There was no coincidence. I was amazed at the details there that I had never heard in all my life as many times as I heard the story or as much as I was connected to church. I thought to myself, this is way more interesting than the kids' stories I read to Ben, so I excitedly told him I found a much better, more detailed version of his favorite Bible story, and we both eagerly listened to it and have listened to the DAB together ever since. Don't worry about it being age appropriate. The Lord will filter it for you. Your kids will not receive what they should not or be exposed to things they shouldn't. The Lord will work it out completely; you need not worry and control it.

For example, the things they don't understand will go over their head, or they will be distracted by something during a particular part. Do not fear explaining things to them when they ask questions. They will ask the right questions that the Lord leads them to ask, and God will help you with your responses, too.

Don't hesitate to ask God to give you the correct response. Read to them the scripture on the armor of God, (Ephesians 6:10-18), and explain to them it is not just saying you are putting it on that matters, it is how you live your life when you are only operating in truth; you are wearing the belt of truth.

When Jesus is the Lord of your life, you are then wearing the helmet of salvation, etc. Pick out a verse about coming against fear. Teach them to speak it out whenever they are scared and tell them it acts like a sword in the spirit and slices the enemy (Hebrews 4:12) because it is the Word of God. We are also using our tongue when we do that. The Bible says life and death is in the tongue (Proverbs 18:21).

Teach them how to fight off the bad dreams and the scary things at night while trying to sleep. Teach them that they do not need to go back into a bad dream. They can wake up and tell the enemy, "I refuse to think of those scary things you are putting in my mind." Then replace those thoughts and topics with good thoughts and memories.

Encourage your kids to revisit good memories. That is where they want to be. Tell them to direct their mind away from the scary thought and not allow it. If you think about it, when focusing on the scary thought, you invite yourself back into the nightmare. You must be intentional. I had to teach Ben to do this independently without me because we have a blended family, and he would go back and forth between households where they did not go to God for such things. I would give him ideas of what to think about in case he was too frozen with fear to think. I would say, "Remember that time we had played catch and got over 100 catches without dropping the ball? Go back there and relive that fun!"

Go through the Bible in a year with your kids multiple times. I started when Ben was five and continued until he was eight and then took a break and listened to other Godly input, and he started requesting it again. Now he is nine, and we still listen to the DAB, but not every day because God has led us to use our time and prioritize what He tells us to do.

We often end up listening to others (pastors, teachers, warriors for Jesus) who are teaching and sharing how alive our God is and how to live in our identity as sons and daughters, heirs to the throne in Heaven. Walking in sonship is an important topic that the Lord told me to pay attention to. God will put it in your children's hearts to want to listen to His Word. Even if their souls start complaining, lay down the ground rules. You are the parent. Woe to the child who did not get disciplined by their parent (Proverbs 18:24).

Chapter 2
Speaking Prayers
and the Word of Your Testimony

Praying Aloud

Pray in front of your kids. Pray out loud. It is okay to have childlike prayers. God is not judging your prayers; He is happy to receive them from you. He wants you to talk to him. He wants to hear from you. Pray in a conversational style in front of your kids, they won't judge you. Speak to God the way you would lovingly speak to your children. It is natural, and they will start to do it with you. Prompt them and ask them to add their prayers. Share testimonies with them and point out when prayer is answered! Testify to others in front of them.

A few months after I started listening to the DAB, and after listening to the prayers at the end, I was so encouraged by all the believers around the world praying for each other that I decided I was going to also do that and encourage people by praying for others and calling it in. I would write down the prayers and call them in. As I did, I noticed that things came to mind to put in the prayer that I would not have put in if I was not writing it down. I noticed it was a phenomenon and realized this has something to do with why people write in journals.

I was not one to journal, but I decided I would start one day. For now, I was happy to see this phenomenon manifesting in my prayers. Then, after a few months, time got crunched, and I came to a point where the words of another came back to my remembrance, and I said, "OK, Lord, I am going to trust that you will help me say the words I need to say since this would remove that journaling phenomena."

I started praying and recording it without writing it down first. I knew that God loved childlike prayers, and I knew that God would help the words flow from me the way they flow when writing them down if I would trust Him to.

I was excited to experience that happening. It was more a fear of man or pride that was driving me to want to write them down first. I didn't know at the time that it was the Holy Spirit that prompted me to take that step of faith and pray on demand.

I didn't repent with words in a prayer for that fear of man or pride, but I did repent. I didn't know I was repenting, but I was repenting with my actions. I changed directions, I changed my ways, and started praying out loud without writing it down. This repentance with my actions was new to me. I didn't realize it was repentance at the time. Once I crossed that road, I was free to call in the prayers on the fly and did it while driving with Ben in the car. He was five at the time.

One day, he was listening to a prayer request air, and he said, "Mom, aren't you going to pray for that person?"

He was truly listening. I knew that was the Holy Spirit speaking through my child, so I said, "Yes," and I did. I called in and submitted a prayer. We did that a few times, and then Ben wanted to start recording prayers, too. I would start, and then he would pray before we ended the call. Then he told me one day, "Mommy, you don't speak. I want to do it." He would call in and pray for people on his own. I was amazed watching the Lord working in and through my child.

Your Testimonies

Let your kids hear you tell others about what God is doing and where you see the Lord moving and working. Start with the small things, and soon, God will give you big testimonies. Let them see you evangelize; let them see you be bold for Jesus! Depending on what age they are, they might help you to be bold, too! Take them with you, don't leave them at home. They are little sponges. They will soak it all in. Even if they don't look like it, they are soaking it in. Do it while running errands, do it during your everyday routine.

Do it in small spurts and, for example, small doses so they can see it is easy. Let them see it doesn't have to take much time. It will build them up; it will teach them how to handle the questions that arise when you do it. It also taught me that it doesn't take that much time.

Once I started doing it, I realized that I had this sort of mental block about it, thinking, "I don't have time right now; I have places to be, things to do, responsibilities to get home, make dinner, get the kids ready for bedtime, etc."

Then, when I started, "I realized I *do* have time to do this." It didn't take up much time at all. That idea was all in my head. I also realized that it is one of my responsibilities and that I need to prioritize it.

Evangelizing with our kids will teach them how to plant seeds and then leave those seeds to be watered and cared for by God through others. They will see the development and what comes of it, and they will get to see the harvest sometimes as well! They will then understand what it means to see the fruit of your labor.

Chapter 3
Worship with Your Children

Expose your children to worship. Don't let them choose not to participate by playing games, listening to their music with headphones on electronics, or by playing in a different area or another room. They need to soak in the presence of God.

Find worship that brings you into his presence and play it for your children; spend time there together. Find a local gathering where the spirit of the Lord is flowing through the worship and is free to move.

I thought I knew what worship was until I was drawn to our church, The Family Worship Center in Lansdale, PA. While they worship, there is a microphone available, and people are free to go up and share encouragements, exhortations, testimony, and prophecy. Then I started tuning into the Sandhills Ecclesia, Dr. Ron, and Adina Horner's virtual church weekly. I found that their worship is very different but similar because the Spirit of the Lord is also free there to move and speak through people. They worship almost completely through testimony, exhortation, and prophecy with minimal music.

I've come to an understanding that true worship is not all just musical; it is free-flowing and different every time. It is not something you can just put on like a production. It requires participation, of you and the people in the congregation.

Let your kids see you worshiping, expose them to engaged worship, and allow them to participate in it by participating yourself. Let them see you surrendering to the Lord in your singing, testifying and sharing, dancing, motions, swaying, and raising of hands. Let the spirit of the Lord bring you to motion.

If you envision yourself doing something like dancing with flags and streamers, then go step out in faith and dance! This happened to me; I saw myself holding streamers and worshiping and flowing with the music. I shared this vision with another woman of God in our church, thinking she would be encouraging and help me to step out in my faith, but instead she completely discouraged me and told me that it would be distracting to people in so many words. She said it would call people's attention to me and off the Lord and ruin the spirit. I knew she meant well but was speaking out of fear that the special thing we have going on in our church would get messed up. I also saw the religious spirit there. I tried my best to end the conversation quickly and simultaneously rebuked it, but it was hard not to get into a division over it and not to be discouraged.

I told myself I would not let the enemy discourage me, and I would step out in faith one day and do the flags because I saw my spirit doing it.

However, I struggled with wanting to avoid her, with the fear of man and defiance all at once. I had to check myself and make sure that my new understanding of dancing with flags or streamers would now come out of worship and not defiance or stubbornness to do it to spite this woman.

I recognized this was the religious spirit working on both sides—working in her and working in me! I didn't want the enemy to gain ground, so I invited the Lord into the situation. Then, in Sunday school one day, the teacher gave an example I could translate over to this situation, and he said, "So what do you do? Love them through it." Once I made the connection to this situation, once the Lord revealed the connection to me, I said to myself and God, "Yes, I want to love her through this! I love her through this!" and all of that just melted away. I could release her to God and move in worship as the spirit lead. I didn't realize it then, but I realized afterward that I was watching my spirit dance. I knew the Lord was calling me and others deeper into worship in our church. Your kids will come to dance with you. I find it much easier to dance when the little ones are around because then the dance does not need to be anything other than childlike motion, which is exactly how we are to enter the Kingdom (Matthew 18:3), with childlike motion and actions.

On a recent Sunday, I saw my spirit dancing again with streamers. I was thinking, "Oh man, I haven't purchased any yet!" but I knew I should be dancing and flowing in that way, so I decided to move my arms and hands as if I had streamers or a flag in my hand. I did not have to be creative. I just followed what I saw my spirit doing. It was easy. As I did, I felt the Lord moving, coming, and flowing. I had my eyes closed, but then, for some reason, I opened them just in time to see another woman in our church take off and start to run! She ran around the entire sanctuary, and I knew that this act of worship and obedience was taking us deeper into the presence of God, and it wasn't just affecting me. That was not the first time someone ran during worship at our church, but it was the first time I witnessed it.

Remove the musical input from your children that does not have heavenly messages. Remove *all* the input that does not have heavenly messages, for that matter! Our kids have enough lies being spoken to them and over them. They do not need negative things to be played repeatedly in their heads. Even if they are not claiming those words or thoughts over themselves in that moment, the enemy will remind them of those things when they are feeling low. Then, they will relate to it and claim the enemy's lies over themselves instead of claiming and standing on the promises of God and what God says about them. Teach your children to look up and stand on the promises of God in the Bible (2 Peter 1:4-10).

Chapter 4
Speak Spirit to Spirit

Speak spirit to spirit with your children. Tell them, "Let's speak spirit to spirit. We invite our spirit and Holy Spirit into this conversation." Ask your children, "Does your spirit need help with anything?" Listen to their answer. Respond to what comes to your mind. When you ask your spirit to engage in the conversation, your spirit, which is connected and intertwined with the Holy Spirit, will respond, and the thoughts that come to your mind will be of the spirit. 1 Corinthians 2:16 tells us:

We have the mind of Christ.

Pray out loud together over whatever the prayer need is and keep it in prayer throughout the coming weeks. If they say they don't know or don't have an answer, ask them what they think might be going on with their spirit. Ask them if they see anything or have any ideas. Then, invite Jesus into the situation. You will be surprised at what happens. Tell them to look around and see if they can see Jesus there. Pray with them about whatever comes up and ask the Lord to show you what to do. This is where the Lord will sometimes engage our imaginations.

Listen for two or three minutes and wait to see what comes to your mind or your child's mind. Share with each other and judge it. What would Jesus do? If it is not harmful or hurtful but is outside your norm, that's okay; do it with childlike faith. Through this experience, the Lord has taken us through many breakthroughs and taught us that these are all methods of spiritual warfare. Each step mentioned in previous chapters is spiritual warfare.

When you speak spirit to spirit and ask what is going on with your or your child's spirit and what it needs, find a scripture related to the response, then read it aloud. Find a word related to what was brought up and search in Google for scripture or in a Bible app, or the concordance, and find verses that have to do with that.

For example, if they just see black or darkness, look up the word *dark* or *darkness*, or *empty* or *walls* or *veils*. Anything that comes to your mind about darkness or what is related to the darkness. Read the verses that come up to your child out loud. Ask them which one stands out to them, and ask yourself, too. If you agree, go with that one; if you don't agree, read both. Go with your hunches. You will be amazed at yet another phenomenon where you know which verse is highlighted by the Holy Spirit working with your spirit. Go to the section in the Bible that the verses are from and read the entire section to your child out loud.

While you are reading, something might make sense to you. It might not seem related, but there is a lesson to learn here or a moral to the story. Speak that out loud and share it with your child. Ask yourself what the relevance to this scripture is or what is this portion of the scripture saying. How does it apply to us in life? Ask yourself and share your answer with your child. Ask your child if they have any ideas on how it applies or what it means. Let them share with you what they think.

Then, ask them if their spirit is feeling better. It is amazing how reading scripture, no matter what Holy Spirit leads you to say it means, does something in the spirit for you and your child. This is a breakthrough. You might not realize it yet, but you will see in no time a breakthrough happening, or you will realize that God answered a question that you had been asking Him through this like He did for me.

The first time we asked our spirits how they were doing was around March 2022. I didn't know Ben could see in the spirit until after we started speaking spirit to spirit. I encourage you to step out in faith, try it, and see what the Lord wants to do. I asked Ben, "Hey, do you want to try this out and speak spirit to spirit?"

He answered, "Yes."

I didn't know how it would work. I was experimenting. First, I asked if his spirit would like to go first. I was thinking, well, he is a kid. He might come up with something to talk about because I had no clue how to start off speaking spirit to spirit. He said, "No." So, I started praying God help me with this! Help me come up with what to say to start this conversation. I was thinking, "Well, I'm the mom, so my spirit must know more than his does." I thought, "Due to experience, maybe my spirit could help his with something." So, I said out loud, "Okay, we agree to speak spirit to spirit so, Ben's spirit, is there is anything my spirit could help you with?"

I was going on faith that I would know what to do or say next, and that by stating that I was going to speak from my spirit, and then just speaking, meant my spirit was there talking through me. My spirit would be able to help or respond. I was going off the only way my imagination could think to do, and I was following advice that I could piece together from Arthur Burk in the free audio section of his website, TheSLG.com.

He has a few albums there that I had listened to on nurturing and developing your spirit when I sought to learn more about the gifts of the Spirit in early February 2022. This was a huge leap of faith, but the pressure was off because I was working with a seven-year-old, my seven-year-old. If it didn't work out, I planned to tell him, "I'm still figuring this out and learning. That must not be the way you do it." But I didn't have to say any of that. When I asked Ben's spirit if there was anything I could help him with, without hesitation or having to pause to think of a response, he said, "Yes, could you please help get rid of this ADHD thing?"

This was amazing because Ben had no clue what to say a minute ago when I asked him if he wanted to go first. Also, Ben had recently been diagnosed with ADHD, and I was struggling with coming into agreement with the prescribed medication. The Lord had told me it was okay for now; it was only for a short time.

I knew then, when Ben's spirit asked me to help him get rid of the ADHD thing, that this was confirmation that ADHD was a spiritual thing. It confirmed all at once that ADHD is connected to the spiritual; our attempt to speak spirit to spirit is a success. His spirit, which is part of the spiritual realm, would know if it was a spiritual problem or not.

Additionally, there is no way my seven-year-old would have asked that question because he thought it was physical, hereditary, and genetic, and you could not ever get rid of it (and he told me so when I tried earlier to tell him Jesus said he was going to be healed of it soon). He was repeating with confidence what he was taught by the doctor and other adults in his life.

Lastly, I knew this was connected, and God was taking us on a journey to an understanding and an answer to my question about the relationship between the spiritual, the natural (physical), and mental illness and medication.

Before Ben was diagnosed, I was already seeking to understand mental illness and the connection to the spiritual realm and generational curses and the relationship between the spiritual realm and hereditary genetics.

When he was diagnosed, I knew that this was connected to my seeking. I knew it was a spiritual attack on my child, but that God was going to use it to bring me to an understanding of what he wanted to teach me and how he was going to answer my seeking. I didn't know how it was going to play out. *I didn't know that speaking spirit to spirit had something to do with it.*

One day, I realized Ben could see his spirit, and I asked him, "What does it look like? Does it look like a boy, like you? Your size?" He said, "Yes." I asked, "Does his face look just like yours? He said, "I can't tell Mom; he's not still; he is always doing backflips!"

I had been seeking to learn about the gifts of the Spirit, and I was led through one of these acts of the Holy Spirit to listen to *Developing and Nurturing Your Spirit* from TheSLG.com. Due to that exposure and my experiences with God, Jesus, and Holy Spirit, I could comprehend what Ben was telling me and experiencing. It was from the spirit realm, was a part of himself, was Godly, and was true, not untrue.

One day, I asked him, "Ben, you said you see my spirit there with you all the time. What is my spirit doing?"

And he told me, "Mom, your spirit is always walking around with a bag over her head." And every time he would take it off, an airplane would come and drop another one on my head so I couldn't see. But he said, "Don't worry! It's like a paper bag; you can still breathe!"

I was shocked. I also knew that I could not see in the spirit like he does, so there was truth in what he was saying. I asked his spirit to help me and my spirit out.

He said, "I already did, Mom." Then, he told me he made a device to keep them from coming over my head. It was some spiritual device that automatically shot a laser at the bag every time it covered my head and disintegrated the bag. I thanked him but knew that this was just a bandage, and I would need to keep seeking God to understand what was happening.

We made it a habit of checking on our spirits, and we learned about the different portions through the *Developing Your Spirit* teachings by Arthur Burk. So, we would check on each portion of our spirits: Prophet, Servant, Teacher, Exhorter, Giver, Ruler, and Mercy. We would say, "Prophet portion, are you here? Teacher portion, are you here? Exhorter portion are you here?" and so on.

We would then have a sense of yes or no to the question. For me, I get a heart feeling or a knowing. Ben can see the portions and if they are there or not. We wrote down the one(s) that were missing or not present or weak and then asked, "What do you think is going on with Prophet?" or whichever portion was missing.

Once, we checked on our spirits, and Ben's spirit was missing every portion. They were not present or responsive. This was a first. Usually, all his spirit would be present, and I would be the one with missing portions. I asked Ben if he had any idea what could be going on with his spirit because I had no clue. I invited Jesus into the situation and asked Him and the angels to help us retrieve his spirit. When all else fails, you must send Jesus and the angels and put it in Jesus's capable hands.

At first, Ben said he had no clue. Then he said, "Wait! I know where my spirit is!"

I was relieved. He said, "A portion is in the east, a portion is in the northeast, a portion is in the northwest, a portion is in the west, a portion is in the southwest, a portion is in the south, and a portion is in the southeast."

I thought, "Oh no! Now, what do we do? How could we possibly retrieve his spirit from there?"

I pulled up my Olive Tree Bible App and did a word search. It made me think of the saying, *"the four corners of the earth,"* so we looked up the word "corners." When we read through the verses, I asked him which one stood out to him, and he said, "You know, Mom. I didn't think I knew, but God has been teaching me and stretching me through this." I said, "Okay, is it the scripture where he is talking about the sheet coming down with the food on it?"

Ben looked at me and said, "Yes, of course!"

I was glad I was on the right track. That was Acts 10:9-33, and I read that section out loud and thought that was good enough. Ben said, "Mom, you didn't finish reading. Read to the end of the chapter." I recognized that this was the Holy Spirit speaking through him, so I continued and read Acts 10:34-4:

> [9] *The next day as Cornelius's messengers were nearing the town, Peter went up on the flat roof to pray. It was about noon,* [10] *and he was hungry. But while a meal was being prepared, he fell into a trance.* [11] *He saw the sky open, and something like a large sheet was let down by its four corners.* [12] *In the sheet were all sorts of animals, reptiles, and birds.* [13] *Then a voice said to him, "Get up, Peter; kill and eat them."*

[14] "No, Lord," Peter declared. "I have never eaten anything that our Jewish laws have declared impure and unclean."

[15] But the voice spoke again: "Do not call something unclean if God has made it clean." [16] The same vision was repeated three times. Then the sheet was suddenly pulled up to heaven.

[17] Peter was very perplexed. What could the vision mean? Just then the men sent by Cornelius found Simon's house. Standing outside the gate, [18] they asked if a man named Simon Peter was staying there.

[19] Meanwhile, as Peter was puzzling over the vision, the Holy Spirit said to him, "Three men have come looking for you. [20] Get up, go downstairs, and go with them without hesitation. Don't worry, for I have sent them."

[21] So Peter went down and said, "I'm the man you are looking for. Why have you come?"

[22] They said, "We were sent by Cornelius, a Roman officer. He is a devout and God-fearing man, well respected by all the Jews. A holy angel instructed him to summon you to his house so that he can hear your message." [23] So Peter invited the men to stay for the night. The next day he went with them, accompanied by some of the brothers of Joppa.

[24] They arrived in Caesarea the following day. Cornelius was waiting for them and had called together his relatives and close friends. [25] As Peter entered his home, Cornelius fell at his feet and worshiped him. [26] But Peter pulled him up and said, "Stand up!

I'm a human being just like you!" [27] *So they talked together and went inside, where many others were assembled.*

[28] *Peter told them, "You know it is against our laws for a Jewish man to enter a Gentile home like this or to associate with you. But God has shown me that I should no longer think of anyone as impure or unclean.* [29] *So I came without objection as soon as I was sent for. Now tell me why you sent for me."*

[30] *Cornelius replied, "Four days ago I was praying in my house about this same time, three o'clock in the afternoon. Suddenly, a man in dazzling clothes was standing in front of me.* [31] *He told me, 'Cornelius, your prayer has been heard, and your gifts to the poor have been noticed by God!* [32] *Now send messengers to Joppa, and summon a man named Simon Peter. He is staying in the home of Simon, a tanner who lives near the seashore.'* [33] *So I sent for you at once, and it was good of you to come. Now we are all here, waiting before God to hear the message the Lord has given you."*

[34] *Then Peter replied, "I see very clearly that God shows no favoritism.* [35] *In every nation he accepts those who fear him and do what is right.* [36] *This is the message of Good News for the people of Israel—that there is peace with God through Jesus Christ, who is Lord of all.* [37] *You know what happened throughout Judea, beginning in Galilee, after John began preaching his message of baptism.* [38] *And you know that God anointed Jesus of Nazareth with the Holy Spirit and with power. Then Jesus went around doing good and healing all who were oppressed by the devil, for God was with him.*

³⁹ "And we apostles are witnesses of all he did throughout Judea and in Jerusalem. They put him to death by hanging him on a cross, ⁴⁰ but God raised him to life on the third day. Then God allowed him to appear, ⁴¹ not to the general public, but to us whom God had chosen in advance to be his witnesses. We were those who ate and drank with him after he rose from the dead. ⁴² And he ordered us to preach everywhere and to testify that Jesus is the one appointed by God to be the judge of all—the living and the dead. ⁴³ He is the one all the prophets testified about, saying that everyone who believes in him will have their sins forgiven through his name."

⁴⁴ Even as Peter was saying these things, the Holy Spirit fell upon all who were listening to the message. ⁴⁵ The Jewish believers who came with Peter were amazed that the gift of the Holy Spirit had been poured out on the Gentiles, too. ⁴⁶ For they heard them speaking in other tongues and praising God.

Then Peter asked, ⁴⁷ "Can anyone object to their being baptized, now that they have received the Holy Spirit just as we did?" ⁴⁸ So he gave orders for them to be baptized in the name of Jesus Christ. Afterward Cornelius asked him to stay with them for several days. (NLT)

After we read to the end of the story, Ben's spirit was completely restored and fully present. We knew by checking and asking the same question: Prophet, Servant, Teacher, Exhorter, Giver, Ruler, and Mercy. We would say, "Prophet portion, are you here? Teacher portion, are you here? Exhorter portion are you here?" and so on.

I was so relieved and surprised that it was that easy. It was confirmation that speaking the Word of God out loud does something in the spiritual realm. It is a sword; it fights the battle for us in the spiritual realm. It was so awesome to get this kind of confirmation! It was also confirmation to us that God is doing a new thing because, in the story, God was telling Peter that he was doing a new thing.

God was saying through this that this type of spiritual warfare that what we were doing, applying, and believing was of God was what God wanted to teach us.

Then, he took it further by having us finish the rest of the chapter. God is saying this is not just for us. This is for the people. This is for his people. They need to know how to fight battles in this new way of speaking to our spirits, searching and seeking to know our spirits, and then using our spiritual sight, sense, and imaginations along with the Word of God to fight the battles to bring the breakthrough.

Look for Related Bible Stories

This brings me to another way to address what is going on with your child's spirit. You can do this by finding a Bible story with something related and then declaring his goodness and victory from the story over their lives and situations.

For example, while driving and on our vacation, I suggested to my kids that we should check our spirits and see how they are doing. I asked them each if they felt their spirits were good or if they could use a little help. They each said they could use a little help.

I knew one of them was struggling with some depression. I asked my son first what he thought was going on with his spirit. He said he saw chickens. The other kids started to chime in and describe the scene or what they saw; they added a temple.

It didn't make sense to me, and we were driving, so I couldn't look up a Bible verse or do a word search in the Bible.

I asked the kids to think of a Bible story with a temple. They didn't think of one, so I said, "Okay, think of one with farm animals in it."

I was praying and asking God to help me with this one because I didn't want to pull over to do a word search.

They said, "Well, what about David and Goliath? David was a shepherd boy."

So, I went with it. I started with David in the field with the sheep and relied on the Holy Spirit to help me take them through the story and whatever moral of the story they needed to hear. It turned out to be about identity.

I told how David was obedient and left his flock and took food to his brothers on the battlefield. When he asked his brothers about what was going on, they told him that he was just a kid and to be quiet and stop meddling. The king also told him he was too young; he was just a boy, but David knew who he was and who his God was and stood up for himself. He knew that God was with him, and he then continued and defeated the giant.

I told them, "Don't let anyone tell you who you are. You stand on what God says about you and don't listen to others picking on you and telling you that you are not good enough to do something. You can do all things through Christ who strengthens you (Philippians 4:13) ."

Then, when I took it to the end of the story, I prophesied over them and blessed them. I will then ask them what happened to David in his life? What is the rest of the story? Asking them gets their wheels turning, and it also gets their engagement and their agreement. And then I will tell them the positive thing(s) that happened.

David was blessed for standing up for himself and who he is in Christ and for being obedient and standing up for God; he became a mighty man of God. He was a mighty warrior, a great ruler and leader, he was very prosperous and had an inheritance to leave for his kids. And then I would turn that into a blessing and prophecy over them and speak it into their lives.

I would say something like, "What does this mean? You, too, are going to be mighty warriors with many great victories. You, too, will be amazing rulers and leaders, and you will have everything you need and then some, enough to bless your generations."

I thought to myself, "Where did that come from?" I realized I did what Arthur Burk does in his book *Blessing Your Spirit with the Blessings of Your Father and The Names of God*. I did not set out to do that. I just did it! My spirit did it; it just came pouring out of my mouth. You can do this too!

I did not have that in mind when we started, but that was a pretty good message for them, especially in this day and age. Then I asked them how their spirits were feeling, if they felt better, and they all said they were better! We didn't have to seek each child individually. That one story helped them all out. Sometimes it works like that; sometimes, we must seek for each one individually. The amazing thing is that it always does something that helps them. We don't know exactly what or how the Word of God does something in the spiritual realm; we just know it builds something for the Kingdom of God, and there is fruit! The depression was gone!

If you find yourself with a visual like volcanos, dinosaurs, portals, or doors, then walk through it verbally with them. Ask, "What do you see? Describe it for me."

Invite Jesus into the situation with you verbally, ask for angelic assistance and come up with some way to get victory using your imagination. Go to a heavenly lab and make spiritual weapons or find a war room on your mountain and use the weapons there to defeat whatever it is or ask Heaven and God to drop bombs from the sky or just command the bombs (in the spirit) to drop from the sky yourself. Defeat whatever is there. Do not stop until you have victory! This works for parents also. It works for everyone! Even if you can't see and you are just guessing or think you are just making it up. You are doing something in the spirit with your imagination.

Then ask how your spirit (or your kid's spirit, or that part of you or them) is feeling. After victory in the spirit/imagination, you will experience victory in the physical/mood realm.

By doing this you are exercising seeing and knowing in the spirit, hearing from God, and exercising your faith. You are warring in the spirit realm. Do a combination of these spiritual warfare tactics if there seems to be a need or you need more confirmation, or if you need to bring it back to the Bible for your own comfort. I did this too.

Chapter 5
A Combined Application

In 2020, a close family friend, whom I called Uncle Randy, was robbed at his home. He was also armed, and there was a casualty. He ended up in prison, and I had no idea what to think or pray. I didn't know what had happened; I was at a complete loss. He went without a trial and bail for two years.

Finally, in March 2022, his first trial came up. I traveled with Ben to my parent's house to go to the trial and be supportive. Ben and I were sitting at the dining room table, and my mom was in the kitchen bouncing around doing mom stuff, and she said to us, "Let's pray for Uncle Randy's trial so he can get out of prison."

Ben's ears perked up. He was seven at the time and wanted to pray, too, but first, he wanted to know the whole story of what was going on and why Uncle Randy was in prison. I hadn't told him about any of it because I didn't know what to say or think. I didn't know how to explain it to him, and I didn't think it was necessary as he was only five or six at the time. Since my mom spilled the beans, I waited for her to summarize for him what the situation was and what we were praying about. I knew she had a way of speaking to children and is gifted at putting things in their terms. How she put it was that Uncle Randy was being falsely accused of preconceived murder instead of self-defense. I knew there was no preconceived murder, so I agreed with this and was grateful for this perspective.

I was having trouble knowing how to pray about this. I did pray throughout the time he was in prison, but my prayer then was, "Lord, I don't know what to think, so I pray that your will be done and that you do a work in Uncle Randy's life."

I could see the Lord was answering that prayer because Uncle Randy got saved in prison! And he was going through the Bible in a year with the DAB! He was using *The One Year Adventure with the God of Your Story*, by Brian Hardin, which I sent him in the mail, and he was going through it with my Aunt Carolyn, who was also a relatively new believer.

Once we established what Uncle Randy needed prayer for, and partly because I didn't know how to pray for him, I suggested that we first check on his spirit to see how it was doing and if there was anything we could help his spirit with.

We understood that our spirits are not connected to time and space and that we could worship or pray with someone in the spirit even when we were not physically together. Just like if you can't join a prayer meeting that you know is going on, you say, "I will be there in spirit and will be praying along with you while you are there."

Immediately, Ben said, "I see prison walls!" I said, "Yes, buddy, he is in prison, but we are seeking about what is going on in the spirit and how his spirit is doing, not what is going on in the physical."

He said, "Yes, Mom, I know! I see prison walls in the spirit! His spirit is in prison!"

I said, "Okay, we invite Jesus into this situation with us." Then I said, "I have a spiritual weapon that we can use!" I had thought up a spiritual weapon to use the day before for something we were praying about, but I didn't get to use it because Ben's spirit didn't need any help at that time. He had made a weapon, solved the problem, and got to victory all with Jesus and hardly any interjection from me that time.

I thought, "Well, I have this spiritual weapon now, I can save it for later use." My spiritual weapon was thought up based on a toy Ben got from the gumball machine at the diner, *Nifty Fifties*, where we ate dinner the night before. It was a hook that you put on the wall to hang things. It looked like a keychain with a loop that swiveled and had a square of adhesive that you use to fasten it onto the wall to hang something, or it could be for the back of a cellphone to put your finger through and carry it.

When I saw it, I thought, "Oh, look at that weapon. You can plug it into a wall, turn it, and then it you'll bore a hole in the wall!" I decided it was an excellent time to use that weapon. I prophetically grabbed the spiritual weapon and tacked it onto the imaginary prison wall I could not see. I was doing this by faith, following the lead of what Ben has done in the past with various prophetic motions, spiritual weapons, and imagination. I described what I was doing with my words and said, "I fasten it to the wall, turn it, and it bores a hole in the wall and..." Ben chimed in and said, "Oh wow!! Mom! Did you see that? The crack went all the way up through the wall!"

This was confirmation again! Ben saw in the spirit what my imagination was doing! I didn't see the wall until just before he said it, but when he said it, my imagination—my mind's eye, saw a bunch of cracks with light shining through them going all through the entire prison wall, and then I saw the wall shattering and crumbling down. So, I said, "Yes!"

Then I described the cracks and the crumbling of the wall, and Ben's eyes got huge, and he said, "Oh man, Mom, you shouldn't have done that!" I knew then that I was seeing in the spirit. I was getting glimpses!

I was so encouraged! But this is the part where the enemy wants to try to get the victory and defeat you. Don't let the enemy win! Don't settle for defeat or a problem you can't solve; you can solve it! We are the ones in charge of our imaginations, and the possibilities are endless!

Ben said, "There were other bad guys (entities) behind those prison walls that should not have been let out, and now they are going to be a problem." By this time, I had this revelation of the imagination, so I said, "Don't worry! It's not going to be a problem. I have another spiritual weapon. It's a vacuum backpack like what the Ghost Busters have. It sucks the bad guys into it, and then we can take them to Jesus for judgment."

Ben was still in panic mode and said, "But there are these different kinds of bad guys. It won't work!"

I said, "Here, I have three backpacks! I made a bunch of them. I just finished making them. One is for you; one is for me, and one is for Grandma!"

I prophetically tossed one to him and one to my mom, and I told him, "You get one type, I will get the other type, and Grandma can get the other type of bad guy!" My mom, praise God, decided to join us, and she prophetically caught the pack, and we both started making noise like we were sucking things up in a vacuum pack.

Ben said, "But the one guy regenerates or reproduces!" He explained that he was some bad guy that he recognized from watching kids play Minecraft on YouTube or something. He is not allowed to play that game, so I was a little upset he was being exposed to that in his dad's house, but I set that aside and said, "That's okay! You know how to defeat him! You work on him, and we will get the other guys!"

Then, Ben declared victory, and we all declared victory and were all rejoicing and praising God. Ben confirmed that he saw in the spirit that Uncle Randy's spirit was free. He said there was a big blue octopus-looking guy still there in a huge cage, and he just saw his tentacle. But, he didn't think he was a bad guy, so we decided to just leave him there. Then he said, "Mom, don't get rid of those bad guys. I want to take them to my heavenly lab and do research on them and see if there is anything there that we can use to make weapons for the Kingdom of God." I smiled and said, "okay."

Later, I read in one of Dan Duval's prayers in his *Prayers that Shake Heaven and Earth* book series that he sent the enemy to Third Heaven places for processing and repurposing. I was amazed that my child had also had this revelation on his own and was implementing it in the spirit. His spirit knew what to do! Since my mom was there and we didn't fully explain all about what God had been teaching us prior to this experience, I felt the need to then, after receiving victory in the realm of the spirit or the imagination, to go to the Bible and see what the Bible had to say about this and Uncle Randy's situation.

We decided to do a word search on the word *prison* and the one that resonated with us was the very first verse that came up, Genesis 39:1-23. It was the story of Joseph and Potiphar's wife, so I went back and read from the beginning and read that section. The chapter was on how Joseph was falsely accused! I knew God was saying Uncle Randy was being falsely accused, just like Joseph was! That is when I knew for sure that Uncle Randy was innocent and was going to get out of prison.

After reading it, I declared the connection and then took it to the end of the story. I did exactly what Arthur Burk does in his blessings book and prophesied based on the rest of the story.

I declared that Uncle Randy was going to get out of prison and that he was going to become a mighty man of God. My mom was so excited and encouraged and could see that this was completely the Holy Spirit working and shared the story with anyone who would listen on her side of the family, not all are believers, and it was a great opportunity to share about God working.

Six months later, he was released—completely free, with all charges dropped. I shared this testimony with another believer, and they said, "It makes complete sense. First, there is victory in the spirit, and then it manifests here on earth." WOW! She had put it into words so clearly. That is exactly what we were learning!

It took me awhile to get the imagination mode down. At first, I thought, "Wow! Ben has a great imagination!" He would always make physical motions to go along with whatever he was doing in the spirit, in his imagination. We always sensed that it was doing something in the spirit and even had some people confirm it through their testifying that they were feeling better, but it wasn't confirmed like this before! I thought, "If nothing else, God is loving what Ben is doing and is getting a kick out of it."

I tried not to discourage him; I was enjoying watching and was tickled that he was using his imagination for the Lord. I didn't say anything like, "Oh, that's not real," or "That's only in your imagination." I went along and played along as best as I could. I was a little saddened that I had always struggled with using my imagination, even as a child, and I was in awe of him.

The Lord showed me that those motions are important. They are prophetic acts that need to be done. That is as far as I understood at the time, but now, I understand more. The prophetic acts need to be done to pull it into the physical realm.

Dr. Ron Horner wrote the *Engaging Heaven* series, and I started reading his book *Unlocking Spiritual Seeing* in August 2022. We were already doing this kind of spiritual warfare, which was an additional amazing confirmation from the Lord and helped me to put words to what was happening and helped connect the dots. It also helped me to understand that the lack of imagination as well as spiritual blindness were not normal or natural. Things are happening in the spiritual realm, affecting our vision and imagination.

Sometime between the time I read the *Commissioning Angels* book and the *Unlocking Spiritual Seeing* book, I began to understand that my imagination was hijacked and under spiritual attack! The enemy is constantly lying to us and twisting the purpose of our imagination to keep us in bondage. In the book *Unlocking Spiritual Seeing*, Dr. Ron goes through Ephesians 1:18-23 in the New King James (NKJV) and in The Passion Translation (TPT) side by side. Verse eighteen is key. In the TPT, it says,

> *I pray that the light of God will illuminate the eyes of your **imagination**, flooding you with light until you experience the full revelation of the hope of his calling—that is, the wealth of God's glorious inheritances that he finds in us his holy ones!*

In the NKJV it doesn't say, *imagination*. It says *understanding*. But when you realize another word for understanding is imagination, the veil gets lifted off our understanding and imagination! It happened to me! I encourage you to read Dr. Ron's book for yourself.[2] I have asked him if I could include a

---

[2] *Unlocking Spiritual Seeing* is available from www.RonHorner.com

chapter of it here because it is so instrumental in this act of worship/spiritual warfare that Ben was doing.

Chapter 6
The Observer Effect

[Taken from Unlocking Spiritual Seeing, *by Dr. Ron M. Horner. LifeSpring Publishing, (2019). Used by permission.]*

In the field of quantum physics, one of the most basic tenets (if not THE most basic tenet) is known as "the observer effect." Simply stated, the observer effect can be defined this way:

What I observe changes what I am observing.

The very act of looking at something causes it to change. Invisible waves of energy or potential change simply by looking at them. As scientists try to measure these waves of energy, they change from waves of energy into a particle (or particles)—something concrete. It is no longer a series of waves—it has become substance. It is something we can observe in our dimension of time and space. It is matter.

Wave Function Collapse

Scientists call this transformation, where the energy waves collapse into a particle, "wave function collapse." It is taking something invisible and making it visible. Something unseen is now seen. We first see it via our imagination using visualization, however.

Within the quantum realm, any possible outcome is available at any and every moment in time.

That is how physicists define it. We need to pause and meditate on that statement. We would call that faith. In Hebrews 11:1:

> *Now faith is the substance of things hoped for, **the evidence of things not seen** [but seen with the eyes of our spirit]* (Hebrews 11:1) (Emphasis mine)

> *Jesus said to him, "If you can believe, **all things are possible to him who believes**."* (Mark 9:23) (Emphasis mine)

Our believing is facilitated by our seeing the matter done via visualization. Visualization is NOT a curse word. It is a valuable technique for accessing the Kingdom realm of Heaven.

> *(As it is written, "I have made you a father of many nations") in the presence of Him whom he believed—God, who gives life to the dead **and calls those things which do not exist as though they did**.* (Romans 4:17) (Emphasis mine.)

You can call those things because you see them with what Paul called the "eyes of your understanding."

> *¹⁷ That the God of our Lord Jesus Christ, the Father of glory, may give to you the spirit of wisdom and revelation in the knowledge of Him, ¹⁸* ***the eyes of your understanding being enlightened;*** *that you may know what is the hope of His calling, what are the riches of the glory of His inheritance in the saints. (Ephesians 1:17-18) (Emphasis mine)*

We have revelation because the eyes of our understanding are made to see (which is what "enlightened" means).

Everything we need, now or in the future, is already available to us. We have this promise:

> *Blessed be the God and Father of our Lord Jesus Christ,* ***who has blessed us with every spiritual blessing in the heavenly places [the unseen realm] in Christ.*** *(Ephesians 1:3) (Emphasis mine) (Additions mine)*

They are unseen to our natural eyes, but not to our spiritual eyes.

> *Grace to you and peace be multiplied in the knowledge of God and of Jesus our Lord; ³ seeing that his divine power* ***has granted unto us all things that pertain unto life and godliness,*** *through the knowledge of him that called us by his own glory and virtue. (2 Peter 1:2-3) (Emphasis mine)*

The ability to see with our spiritual eyes is vital equipment for our walk with God. By spiritually seeing we can tap into the revelation God has for us.

We, in the body of Christ, have been so "Word-oriented" (which is a left-brained function) that we have ignored the understanding of that Word that comes from exercising right-brained function.

Everything we need is available. God has provided *everything*. Our challenge has been in learning how to get what is in Heaven to manifest in the earth. Quantum physics is explaining how things work that the Scriptures have been telling us. These glory waves of potential need to collapse into our reality—into our realm of time and space. What is in Heaven needs to manifest in the earth.

> *It is by faith we understand that the world was fashioned by the word of God, and **thus the visible was made out of the invisible**. (Hebrews 11:3) (Moffatt)[3] (Emphasis mine)*

---

[3] The Bible: James Moffatt Translation by James A R Moffatt, Kregel Publications, Grand Rapids, Michigan, USA, 1994

> *What is unseen*
> *needs to become seen.*

Scientists refer to this phenomenon of the invisible becoming visible as "wave function collapse;" this is what happens when we pray. The unseen becomes seen.

> *We see it with our spirit, then we can*
> *see it in the natural arena.*

Give us this day our daily bread. (Matthew 6:11)

The provision that is in Heaven manifests in the earth through food, water, finances, etc. That is *why* we pray.

If I am sick, I look at what the Word says about my situation, "by His stripes I was healed,"[4] and as I grasp what He has said concerning me—as I see it with the eyes of my heart, my situation changes. I go from sickness to health. I "see" it (I observe it) and the situation changes—wave function collapse.

As we see with our spiritual eyes, we see what Heaven sees about me. Heaven's version of me is of a person healed, whole, glorious, without weakness or illness dominating my body. As I see that, I am changed.

---

[4] 1 Peter 2:24

> *But we all, with unveiled faces, beholding as in a mirror the glory of the Lord, are being transformed into the same image from glory to glory, just as by the Spirit of the Lord. (2 Corinthians 3:18) (Emphasis mine)*

My observation (seeing with my spirit) will result in transformation!

What is potential in Heaven collapses into this realm, and I become what is Heaven's version of Me.

> *If then you were raised with Christ, **seek [observe] those things which are above**, where Christ is, sitting at the right hand of God. ² Set your mind [your sight] on things above, not on things on the earth. ³ For you died, and your life is hidden with Christ in God. ⁴ When Christ who is our life appears, then **you also will appear with Him in glory [in a transformed state of being]** (Colossians 3:1-4) (Emphasis mine) (Additions mine)*

That is why we put off the things that hinder our transformation. Let us read a little further:

> *Therefore, put to death your members which are on the earth: fornication, uncleanness, passion, evil desire, and covetousness, which is idolatry. ⁶ Because of these things the wrath of God is coming upon the sons of disobedience, ⁷ in which you yourselves once walked when you lived in them. ⁸ But now you yourselves are*

> *to put off all these: anger, wrath, malice, blasphemy, filthy language out of your mouth. ⁹ Do not lie to one another, since you have put off the old man with his deeds, ¹⁰ and have **put on the new man who is renewed in knowledge according to the image of Him who created him.** (Colossians 3:5-10) (Emphasis mine)*

Observation brings transformation!

What we observe—manifests.

The works of the flesh Paul just mentioned create the wrong images in our mind—images that bring destruction to ourselves, our relationships, and our lives.

We must behold
that which is life-giving,
not death producing!

Jesus said that He did what He saw his Father do and said what He heard his Father say. He observed what his father was doing, agreed with it, and it manifested in the earth.

> *"Again, I say to you that if two of you agree on earth concerning **anything that they ask, it will be done for them** by My Father in heaven. (Matthew 18:19) (Emphasis mine)*

The word "ask" implies a search for something hidden—something desired. Because we come into agreement with Heaven, the hidden becomes manifest in the earth.

> *When you are praying over a matter,*
> *see with your spiritual eyes*
> *what it is you desire.*
> *Once you see it, come into*
> *an agreement with Heaven*
> *so that it can manifest.*

We have made it much more difficult than it is. We need to agree with Heaven; Heaven is waiting on us! When we see via the realm of the spirit, we are visualizing the unseen.

> *The purpose of such visualization*
> *is to cause the unseen*
> *to become seen.*

Once seen in the spirit, begin to release it in the earth by the words of your mouth. Let your mouth agree with what your spirit sees so that it can come forth in the earth; to speak what you do not see is presumptuous.

In the Gospel of Mark, Jesus explains how it works:

> *So, Jesus answered and said to them, "Have faith in God [trust the process God has instituted].* [23] *For assuredly, I say to you, whoever says to this mountain, 'Be removed and be cast into the sea,' and does not doubt in his heart, but **believes [he is able to see with his spiritual eyes the thing desired]** that those things he says will be done, he will have whatever he says [when his words are an expression*

of his agreement with Heaven].[24] *Therefore I say to you, whatever things you ask* ***when you pray, believe that you receive them****, and* ***you will have them****. (Mark 11:22-24) (Emphasis mine) (Additions mine)*

In the last chapter of Luke, Jesus instructs his followers to wait in Jerusalem until they are endued with the power of the Holy Spirit. In Acts 1, He continues the story and explains why. In verse eight, He says they would become witnesses. Witnessing is not so much something we do with our mouth; rather it is the result of seeing with our eyes. When someone says they were an eyewitness to something, it means they observed it with their eyes. Then they told me what they saw.

One of the most credible forms of testimony is eyewitness testimony. The person testifying has seen something and is willing to describe what they saw. As we use the eyes of our heart and observe what is reality in Heaven, that heavenly reality will collapse and change form into the thing needed. At that point, our eyewitness testimony is two-fold. We have seen in Heaven, *and* now we see on the earth.

When I very recently learned much of this from Bible teacher Charity Kayembe in a video,[5] I saw how it could impact everything we do and everything we understand about The Glory! Within the Glory is the unlimited potential of everything

---

[5] Kayembe, Charity. "Hearing God Through Your Dreams – Session 1 – Bridges to the Supernatural." Communion With God Ministries. Teaching.

ever needed on the earth. It is the energy that can be transformed by observing with our spiritual eyes and seeing what God sees and agreeing with that. The Glory is limitless!

Jesus understood this when He stated:

> *All things have been delivered to Me by My Father,* and no one knows the Son except the Father. Nor does anyone know the Father except the Son, and the one to whom the Son wills to reveal Him. (Matthew 11:27) (Emphasis mine)

As we assimilate these concepts (which will be easier to understand from the realms of Heaven), our lives will change, and situations will change—this applies to *every* arena!

[End of chapter insert.]

If you get stuck, you can pause the engagement. You can always pause an encounter or even a memory and then go back to where you left off after prayer. You can always get back there and pick up where you left off. If you pause it, God will keep you safe while you pray and ask God for wisdom and guidance. Pray and ask God for protection. Sometimes, we pray the Opening Prayer[6] from Dan Duval's *Prayers that Shake Heaven and Earth* book, and then when we are done, we almost always pray the Closing Prayer from the *Extreme Prayers that Shake Heaven and Earth* book.

---

[6] See the Appendix

If not, then I pray it at bedtime, or I ask my spirit to pray it along with the angels and put it on a time loop so it is prayed continuously in the heavens—these prayers, among other things, put on the armor of God. I also noticed it shuts down the religious spirit or hinderances to our ability to make progress. It is important to pray out loud.

There are things in the spiritual realm that happen because of our words and the frequencies that our words project. Good words do good and go into the kingdom of God; bad or negative words do bad and give power to the kingdom of darkness/evil. That is why it is very important to always claim victory during these imaginative endeavors. Speak out and declare that the enemy cannot undo the work that you did, your victory. Ask your kids to judge things, like their favorite cartoon hero. Ask where the power comes from. Tell them, if it is not of God, then you are against it. If we only use the power of God, all our imagination tools and weapons are powered up with the power of God. We charge them with the names of God and the Word of God.

There was no detailed list of instructions I had come across to use and study when I started to speak spirit to spirit with my kids or at least I hadn't happened upon any. Arthur Burk gave prompting and nudging in the teachings I was led to, but he directs all his stuff to clinicians. I didn't come from a clinician background, and I had no idea what his audience already knew or could see or anything. I was listening and applying how and where the Holy Spirit led and judged by the fruit, and I said to myself, "Well, I am not a clinician, but I am a mom! So, I still need to listen to this and learn this stuff!"

When Ben and I started journeying and learning, I could see that what was coming out was fruit from a combination of what God was teaching us through Arthur Burk, Dan Duval, and Dr. Ron Horner's ministries.

I did get stuck and didn't know what to do a few times. The first time we paused, I thought of it as a court case in the Courts of Heaven, like how Dr. Ron Horner's ministry shows us to visualize or imagine ourselves stepping into Heaven. I spoke aloud and declared, "We step into the Courts of Heaven; I mean, we are *in* the Courts of Heaven!" I intentionally imagined as if we were already there from the beginning, viewing the encounter as part of the case, and then we needed to pause and discuss it in court. But instead of discussing it in the court, I asked for a pause so we could pray about it, learn more about it, and then come back to it.

I knew you could do it in earthly court, so I knew I could do it in my imagination, which I had learned is connected to the spiritual realm and the heavens. I didn't know the name, so I called it a *pause*. It is formally called a *Continuance*. God is merciful and full of grace. He will honor your request even if you don't know the correct terminology. Heaven will fill in the gaps for you as you go through. I have peace that nothing will move from there until we are ready, and God helps us by teaching us and giving further revelation regarding what to do, how to pray, and what tactic to use.

Now I know in the Courts of Heaven, you can also ask for wisdom and godly counsel and help from Heaven and the court, so you can ask for guidance and wait for the response of what to do to come to you right then and there instead of pausing it! But do whatever you need to do to boost your faith. You can also switch to a different tactic in the middle, from court mode to worship mode, to doing a word search in the Bible.

Chapter 7
Inner Healing

Let's back up to 2020 when I was journeying with God to understand spiritual gifts and generational curses. I was including my son Ben in my journey because he loved Jesus, and when he was with me, I wanted to saturate him with things of God instead of things of this world. He would be within ear shot when I listened aloud to sermons and amazing men and women of God. In 2020 and 2021, it was all audio, and I hardly read any books; In 2022, I started reading books. That is a testimony of healing in and of itself. I will share that in another book someday.

When I read, most times, I read out loud. The Lord showed me that is the best way to process what I am reading. I would also sometimes read the books I was reading out loud, and Ben would hear them. Sometimes, I would read parts of them out loud to him on purpose as the Lord led.

Unbeknownst to me, Ben was to be my partner on this journey, requiring us to learn about and start an inner healing and deliverance journey.

Deliverance material kept finding its way into what I was listening to or reading. I tried to only listen to or read things that the Holy Spirit put in front of me, and I would judge them as I went. I was looking for God speaking through it and looking at the fruit.

At first, I kept setting the deliverance stuff or parts of it aside. I would say, "Ok, Lord, I will take the information out of this that I know you are speaking to me about, (for example, the armor of God); I am just going to set the rest of it aside because deliverance is not my thing."

Eventually, throughout 2020 and 2021 after this deliverance stuff repeatedly came to me from all different sources, I finally got the message that the Lord was leading me to learn about deliverance ministry.

I said, "Okay, Lord, I know if I start learning about this, I will be responsible for the information, and I will have to do something with it.[7] So, I accept that responsibility. Just let me know what you want me to do, and I will do it."

Then, I found that deliverance and inner healing are intertwined, and I realized I was also being called to learn about inner healing.

---

[7] 1 Corinthians 4:1-2

Once, after this realization and a discussion with God, we were checking on our spirits again with a friend of mine and her daughter, who is Ben's age; they were both 8.

When we asked what they thought was going on with her spirit, she said that she found herself standing in pool water. We invited Jesus into the situation with us and asked about the water. Was it good, clean water, or was it yucky? She said it was clean and comforting. She said she was wearing a yellow swimsuit with a butterfly on it. Her mom recognized the swimsuit she described and confirmed that she had one like it when she was five years old. My friend asked her daughter how old she was, and her daughter responded that she was seeing herself as younger, maybe around five.

I knew immediately that this was not just an in-the realm-of-the-spirit experience. Her spirit took us to the trauma where the healing was needed. We were in her subconscious, an area of her heart. I realized that we were brought there to address some kind of trauma and that the Lord wanted to do some kind of inner healing work. This was a part of her soul.

She was a little scared, and she described what she was seeing in her imagination and the spirit realm. She saw doors and walls. She was in a building.

We asked her if she could see Jesus and encouraged her to look for him there. He was there, so she took his hand.

I began to pray and repent for what had happened in that building: any defilement, sins, transgressions, and inequities. We also repented on behalf of ourselves and our bloodlines for any part that we played knowingly or unknowingly and asked that the blood of Jesus cleanse the walls and the entire building and the land it was on.

She said she knew the building. She was there when she was younger, but she couldn't remember. Then she described what was happening as she was seeing in the spirit: Jesus was standing behind her and nudging her forward. He wanted her to walk through the door. So, we encouraged her, too. She saw the same thing in that door. Again, more pool water.

Then they went back through and picked a different door. Again, more pool water. Then Holy Spirit put it in my heart to say, "Look! See, there is nothing here that can hurt you anymore. It is all clean, and the water is clean and nice and comforting. Jesus wants you to know that there is nothing to fear anymore. He wants you to regain these areas inside of you."

Her mom encouraged her to look around and find a box, put all her fear in the box, and give it to Jesus.

She looked a little lost, so I told her Jesus had a box for her, and to get it from Him. She confirmed that Jesus gave her a box.

At that point, we were pulling into her house, but when she was walking out of the car to her house, she was walking very slowly. Then she said I am still in the water. I am still walking through the water, and its dark. I asked her to look around to see if she could still see Jesus. She said no, she gave him the box, and then He left with it. I said, "OK, don't worry. We will not leave you there in the dark or in the water."

We went inside and sat on the couch and did a word search in the Bible for the word darkness, and we came to Micah 7:8-11. We read the entire section, but verse eight stood out to her mom. *"When I fall, I shall rise, when I sit in darkness the Lord will be a light to me." (Micah 7:8)*

She was led by Holy Spirit to tell her daughter that Jesus is always there, and that He wants her to keep looking for him even when she can't see him.

We asked her if she understood, and she said, "Yes," and then she said, "I am okay. I am back now, and safe."

We had no idea then that this kind of spiritual warfare would lead us to the inner healing of soul parts, but that is what happened.

Be sure to then take the time and have your child's spirit ask your spirit if there is anything their spirit can help your spirit with. Do not be concerned with being on the opposite side of it. God will help you through and help you answer the questions and so will your child and their spirit.

Sometimes, I didn't know what was going on, but I knew there would always going to be something, so in faith, I would say, "I don't know, what do you see?" Or, "What do you think is going on with my spirit?" Then we would go from there. If you still have nothing to go by, ask Holy Spirit to tell you, or just take a Bible and open to a random location and read the section.

Don't miss out on this amazing journey for yourself. This goes back to step one. You need to be doing all this too for *yourself* and *your* emotions, spirit, soul, and body. You need breakthroughs just as much as your children do.

Chapter 8
Expanding Past Yourself

Once you get this down, consider applying it to different situations. Expand out past yourself and how your spirit is doing. The example I mentioned in the last chapter expanded out to the soul realm. You can also apply it to the body realm, like health issues, for instance.

To do this, you do the same as described in previous chapters. Just ask a slightly different question, like, "Do you see anything," or "What do you think is going on in the spirit surrounding _____ (name the health issue)?" Then note what you end up seeing, hearing, or experiencing.

You can also apply this to praying over situations, buildings, and even governments. This expansion is brand new to us.

I recently started reading Robert Rodich's book, *Moving Toward Sonship: Becoming Sons of the Father's Design*. He talks about applying our anointing, something all human beings, sons and daughters of the Most-High God have to everyday aspects. He questions, and asks if we have missed its broader applications, and if demonstration or breakthrough can only happen in times of revival. He asked where we can apply the anointing? My spirit understood this and immediately started to branch out per the leading of the Holy Spirit.

Impacting a Strip Club

The other day, we did this for a strip club called *Cloud 9* that we pass on the way to church. We understand that my son, Ben, can see in the spirit well. I am a knower, so I told him, there is some evil keeping this strip club here. There is a Christian radio station that positioned itself right next door. I know that their placement was strategic to come against the strip club.

I have prayed to cleanse the land and repented on behalf of the people, and I know others in the local churches have been praying for this place to shut down for years. Even their kids have been praying since they were kids, and those kids are now adults.

I spoke to Ben and said, "Look around and see if you see anything in the spirit and ask Jesus if He wants to show you anything that will help us pray to shut it down."

Ben is nine years old right now, and he didn't know what a strip club was. He kept on calling it a strip mall. Eventually, he resigned to calling it an *evil strip mall* because he always messed up and didn't call it a club. I gave him the gist of it—a brief description where men watch women dancing and taking their clothes off. I explained how that is sinful because we are not supposed to use our bodies that way, and men are not supposed to use women that way; they are supposed to have relationship with them and show them love and respect and provide for them in a marriage. I also mentioned how some of them are also sinning because they are looking at other women when they have wives and families. That day he did not see anything.

The next time we drove by, two days later, he said he saw that place was packed, although the parking lot was empty. I knew he was seeing in the spirit. He described what he saw, and it was exactly what goes on in a strip club. He said the audience is full of men and the women are on the stage. Then, he said there is a bar that is separate, and it is only for men who like other men (he didn't want to say the word *homosexual*).

We started repenting. We repented for the men and women who were making wrong choices and for the people who influenced them and their bloodlines, ancestors, and generations.

Then he told me the women were dancing and there were poles. He didn't understand how you dance with a pole. I knew he was providing information he was seeing and did not have prior earthly knowledge of it. I wasn't worried because I knew God would filter it and only show him what was okay for Ben to see.

Then Ben asked me how old you needed to be to go in there. I honestly didn't know.

I said, "Probably 21."

He said, "What? Why such a specific age?" I told him it was because that is how old you need to be to drink alcohol.

He said, "Are you sure? Maybe you can go in there to just sit in the audience and not drink."

He had this funny look, and I asked him, "Why are you asking me these questions? Are you trying to go in there to investigate further?"

He said, "NO WAY, Mom!"

Then I knew. I said, "Do you see something? What do you see?"

He said, "Yes, I saw children in there. They were backstage."

He said, "Maybe they are the children of the dancers." He said, "They were watching."

I asked if they were watching the dancers and he said, "Yes, but the dancers are other kids."

I could tell that he had no idea about child trafficking. He was not connecting the dots, which is God's grace, and by then, I had endured enough. I thanked Jesus quietly for taking us through this so we could work together with him to take this place down and for filtering it for Ben.

We immediately started repenting again on their behalf, on behalf of those behind this. I asked for the land, building, and people to be cleaned with the living water and the blood of Jesus and that all the parts of the children would be taken to the Third

Heaven to be reunited with Jesus and healed. We requested search and rescue angels to come and rescue the children, and we commissioned the warring angels.

This time Ben requested the Archangel Michael to come and fight with his armies and he confirmed he was fighting in the war against the devil and there were a bunch of these goblin things the angels were fighting. Then Ben saw a huge bad guy/monster that looked like Godzilla, an evil entity, and then he saw another one that was even more fierce and much bigger, like 200 feet bigger, but this one was on God's side. He was fighting the evil one and defeated it.

We rejoiced in the victory, praised God, and asked for healing for all involved. Now, we are eagerly watching to see what the Lord is going to do and how this is going to manifest in the physical and shut down that strip club, the child exploitation and trafficking. It has been a prayer of mine to help with shutting down trafficking. I always wanted it to shut down and it is also a huge prayer of my Dad, Benny's grandfather, but in 2020, I asked God to show me how to get involved; how I could help, and how my Dad could help.

I knew God's answer was that we needed to battle this in the spirit, but I didn't understand how until now. God is calling us to branch out further and go after the overarching problem or reason there are strip clubs, child exploitation, and trafficking in our area. Like when you pray for someone and bring things to the Courts of Heaven, you repent on behalf of yourself and your bloodlines and make it a class action lawsuit to cover everything at once instead of having three different cases, one for your friend/client one for their sister and one for their parents. Lord, thank you for this journey. Help us to go where you want us to go and do what you want us to do and to be dangerous for Your Kingdom.

What I am learning is that going where God wants us to go and doing what God wants us to do is not always physical, so don't be afraid to seek and ask God what He wants for you and where He wants you to go or be. He will not take you away from your family if your ministry is your family. Most of the time, where He wants you to go, and what He wants you to do is in the spirit.

The Lord has been leading us through this journey and answering prayers all along the way, bringing healing and breakthrough in amazing ways. There will be more books written with testimonies, but I wanted to share more of the ADHD testimony here.

Chapter 9
Hearing God's Voice

Almost a year after speaking spirit to spirit with Ben, in January of 2023, I sat down, got quiet, and took the free class from Dr. Ron Horner's ministry on CourtsNet.com called *Four Keys to Hearing God's Voice*. This is one of the best things I have done!

It got me to sit still, get quiet and listen to what God wants to say to me in that moment. I learned that you don't need to spend hours and hours waiting to hear what God has to say; He answers within a couple of minutes; we need to spend the time, be intentional, listen, and allow Him to speak.

The first thing you do is:

1. Get quiet.
2. Fix your eyes on Jesus.
3. Tune into the spontaneous flow of Holy Spirit. Holy Spirit is like a continuously flowing river. If you listen, you can catch what's happening in the river. It's not always on the topic you hope to hear about.

You need to be open to receive what God wants to talk to you about.
4. Write it down.[8]

How you tune in is that you ask one of these: God, Jesus, Holy Spirit, and Heaven, "What do you have to say to me?" You can ask each of them, spending 10 minutes each if you like, each one will speak to you. When you ask, have a pen and paper in hand and write it down!

Then, you listen and sit quietly; for me it's helpful to put on worship music with no words. My favorite is prophetic piano, played by Adina Horner, Dr. Ron's wife. It's available on YouTube, Spotify, and other music outlets.

Write down what you hear. Sometimes, I see a picture instead, so I write down what I see. After 10 or 15 minutes, check it against scripture and what I know of God's principles, and judge it. Ask, yourself if it came from you, from God, or somewhere else. If you can't tell, ask someone you trust to give you Godly counsel on whether or not they think it came from God or somewhere else.

Remember that you asked God; you didn't invite anyone else. "Simply don't invite anyone else to the party," as Dr. Ron says.

---

[8] Credit goes to Dr. Mark Virkler for unpacking this teaching to the Body of Christ.

Also, remember that if it is accusatory, condemning, brings confusion, discouragement, or destroys, then it is from our soul or the enemy.

What you hear from the Godhead or Heaven will be loving, comforting, edifying, peace-giving, hope-filled, and a blessing. It might be convicting or surprising but in a way that gives direction, not shame, guilt, or condemnation.

During the first week of March 2023, during my time with God after my devotional, I read a little in Dr. Ron Horner's book *Commissioning Angels – Volume 1: Maximizing Your Relationship with Heavenly Hosts*. He talked about how we have heavenly bodies that have no imperfections, and how our souls don't understand this, but our spirits will. He was encouraging us to tell our spirits to reside in our heavenly bodies that are free of all illness and defects and to get comfortable in and operate from them in the Third Heaven. Once our spirits do, then they will be able to bring our souls and physical bodies into alignment and it will then manifest here in this realm.

I was praying about it and then wanted to immediately try it and put it into practice. The best way I have found is to apply what you have learned immediately, and God will show you. You will see good fruit come from it. He will either confirm or He will show you otherwise.

Of course, the enemy wants to deceive, so it requires prayer and discernment, but prayer first because sometimes we think we are using discernment and we are not, we are being shut down by the religious spirit that is presenting itself like discernment, because we did not pray about it first. We just think we know.

Chapter 10
Learning to Hear God's Voice

After doing the hearing from God exercise for about 3 months or so, I still didn't think I was communicating up to par with God, seeing and hearing the way I could if I didn't have a bag over my head in the spirit.

It had been about a year since that experience/understanding and I was seeking God and asking him to help me. I could see God was taking me on a journey to freedom from spiritual blindness which had layers. Part of that was the journey He was taking me on. He was teaching me about the spiritual ties behind Freemasonry and how my family is under that bondage.

After praying over myself and Ben and encouraging our spirits to reside in our heavenly bodies (as mentioned in the previous chapter), I noticed that Ben was not struggling with sitting still. He was not struggling with focusing while reading! He was not showing signs of ADHD!

I was praising God and giving glory to God! I also started telling my friends about it, of course how could I keep it quiet!? I thought that it was the answer to my prayer, but it did not stay. Ben still struggled with focus after that, but I didn't get discouraged. I knew there was something there, we just didn't get it all figured out yet.

In the meantime, I wanted to be able to differentiate between the Father's voice, Jesus's voice, and the voice of the Holy Spirit. I also wanted to hear my own spirit's voice and to be able to differentiate between the voice of my spirit and the voice of my soul and the voice of my body. I wanted to have encounters where we—my spirit, soul, and body would communicate in conversation with each other.

I knew Ben and I were doing this to an extent, but I wanted the version where it was like a movie playing in real time. I knew Ben experienced this so I knew it could be done. Ben is a child, so it made sense to me that it would be easier for him, he has had less time in life to build up walls.

In mid-April 2023, Kendra McDonald, a coach from Bride Ministries, suggested that I do the Hearing God's Voice exercise, but do it at three different times. The first time I am asking God, the Father what He wanted to speak to me that day. Then, waiting 5 minutes, journaling it, and then asking Jesus and journaling it, and finally, asking Holy Spirit and journaling it. I started to do this a few times, making time where I could. I found it very interesting, enlightening, encouraging, and instructive.

I always received some kind of communication from each of them that I would then apply immediately, or I would gain the understanding on later and then be able to apply it. Interestingly as abstract as some of the things were, God always ended up showing me what they meant.

Chapter 11
Heavenly Alignment

Around mid-April 2023, Dr. Ron Horner's Courts of Heaven ministry started discussing creating cooperation between your realms in their weekly Tuesday night LifeSpring Mentorship meeting. I read the blog about it a week later and was introduced to *Heavenly Alignment*.

Dr. Robert Rodich (Doc) taught Dr. Ron's ministry about it, and I was learning about it through them. On May 15th, 2023, I listened to Dr. Ron Horner's church service[9] recorded the week before. During the worship part, there was a testimony from a woman who followed the teachings, aligned her realms, and then asked her body what she needed.

She then shared how her body spoke and told her what nutrients she needed and what to eat to get them. That was the first time I understood that I was to expand on the exercise and

---

[9] RonHorner.com/SE

apply the hearing of God's voice exercise to my spirit, soul, and body. This was God answering my prayer!

I started to understand that when I ask my spirit something, that is who answers. When I ask my soul something, that's who answers. When I ask Holy Spirit something, that's who answers! When I ask Father God something, that's who answers, and when I ask Jesus something, that's who answers! When I ask Heaven something, Heaven answers. When I ask the men or women in white something, one of them answers. I am learning to discern or recognize who I am talking to as I do not see in the spirit as well as my son does, or at least not yet.

For now, I have figured out that when I direct my questions or conversation to a specific being or part of my being, that is who answers. The Lord showed me a Bible verse to help me with this. I like the way Dr. Rodich wrote it in his book where he says, "Please do not fall into the trap of shunning your destiny, your real identity, and the supernatural just because you are afraid you might cross over into the New Age or some other level of error. Do not be afraid to be open to the supernatural side of your walk with Jesus."

Jesus Himself told us that if a child asks his father for an egg, the father will not give him a snake—because the father loves His child and will not give him something bad in response to his sincere request. (Luke 11:12, Matthew 7:9)

Likewise. as you hold tightly to His hand, He will lead you only into truth, even though it might be a truth you have not previously discovered. So then, as I put these insights together and connect the dots, I should be able to talk to my body as it is part of my being and get the true response.

I tried it out the next morning, asking my own body, spirit, and soul what they needed individually. The first thing my body said was, "It needs Heavenly Alignment." When I wrote it down, I had no idea what Heavenly Alignment meant (maybe because the ministry was calling it 'cooperating with your realms' at that time).

I also had completely forgotten about the experience we had a month and a half before with an exercise from Dr. Horner's angels book,[10] where we asked our spirit to help bring our souls and physical bodies into alignment, so our heavenly bodies could manifest on earth.

Little did I know that this has to do with our heavenly blueprint. What Holy Spirit did bring to my mind was about clothing, so I thanked God for covering my body up with more decent clothes because He recently told me to stop wearing tight pants and low-cut shirts and I was obedient and changed my wardrobe.

Previously, I wore a lot of leggings with shirts that stopped at the waist because that is what my husband preferred. I decided to put God's request over my husband's and gradually made the shift.

---

[10] *Engaging Angels in the Realms of Heaven* by Dr. Ron M. Horner (LifeSpring Publishing, (2021))

I also saw a horse's tail from a dark colored horse and layers, in my imagination, which is one way we see in the spirit. I didn't know what to do with this either. I requested protection over my body and proper intimacy with my husband because those were the things that came to mind. I could make some sense of them.

I won't go into it in detail here; let me say the Lord had shown me ways we give power to the enemy without realizing it, and the prayer resulted from that knowledge. I prayed for help to get under the layers of my body or body issues and to be able to address each layer. I asked for wisdom and counsel about each layer.

I also requested the cleaning and purification of my layers, and I asked for His living water to run through them, detailing them, so that the nicks and crannies would be all cleaned out. I didn't see how that related to my body, but it came to my mind, so I prayed out loud.

Next, I asked my soul what it needed, and it said, "Carrots." I didn't think I needed to eat carrots because I was talking to my soul and not my body at the time, so I asked for heavenly nutrients and refreshment for the eyes of my soul, because carrots are for assisting with seeing. I knew my soul did not need the food kind of carrot; that would be my body realm. I still increased my carrot intake though, just in case, and because I liked that it reminded me of this Godly experience.

I also saw a marsh/bog, so I thanked God for the ecosystem in the bog and asked that my ecosystem be renewed and refreshed. Later, I looked up the cranberry bog[11] with Ben, and we did a virtual tour because it was too far away to visit that week. I thought at least looking it up in the physical and teaching Ben about it might be some sort of prophetic act of obedience.

Next, I saw a metal octopus tentacle. I was surprised I saw so much instead of receiving via thoughts or knowing, which was typical for me.

I went into imagination mode, envisioned myself, and declared verbally:

"I pull out the middle octopus tentacle and locate what it is connected to.

Jesus, would you please uproot it? Thank you! I bring it to the altar of the Lord and give it to the Father there as a sacrifice along with the dislodged armor-coated tentacle.

I thought that was going to be the end of it. Then I saw a vision of myself removing a helmet or blinder from over my head. It looked like something that came from a spaceship, and I sensed that this act was opening the lines of communication between my spirit, soul, and body and removing the blinder from over my head.

---

[11] A cranberry bog is a watery area where cranberries are grown, then harvested.

I was thinking about the paper bag Ben had seen over my head, and I knew this was it. It was being removed, although it looked different to me than to him. I thanked my soul for the opening and unlocking so that I could see. I thanked Jesus for the work He was doing. I was working with my soul; my soul did the unlocking with Jesus, but my spirit was the one who was freed from the blinder.

Jesus answered two of my prayers through that encounter and I didn't realize it until I was writing this book! Immediately after I declared that I received nutrients from carrots, Jesus led me to search out my ecosystem (the cranberry bog). In doing this, I was prompted to request that my personal ecosystem be refreshed and renewed. And, that is when the blinder came off my head and eyes! WOW!

I didn't fully understand the encounter or perspective at the time. I did know that my prayer to get to the root of the bag over my head was being answered, and I was excited about that because Ben's little spiritual weapon was more of a temporary bandage. There is a lesson in that, too. Do not get discouraged when you see victory in the spirit and it doesn't stick. You did accomplish something. You just didn't get to the root and need to keep working on the layers.

It's funny that carrots are a root. Oh, how fun God is! This only happened because my soul and spirit worked together, and my soul unlocked my spirit seconds before! That unlocking had to do with getting my realms to cooperate with each other! This was *heavenly alignment*, which my body had requested only minutes before. Just wow! I am in awe.

It also answered my request to see my spirit. I didn't realize at the time I was seeing my spirit. I thought I was just seeing a vision of myself, but it was the spirit part of me. I know this because my spirit had the bag over her head. To be able to see my spirit was something I had put on my vision list for 2023.

My vision list is a list of things God told me He would do, or I see happening, want to happen, or am praying for. These are things that I can't do myself; only God can do them. Being able to see in the spirit that thoroughly was a breakthrough! There is so much more breakthrough that came from this. Eventually, I will show you how it led to the solution to the ADHD problem and mental illness and many other things!

Next, I asked my spirit what it needed, and she said, "my mountain," and I saw big boulders on an incline. I began to speak out loud. I requested heavenly equipment to scale the boulders to bore into them and tap into the mountain, to receive the elements and the resources inside. I was using my imagination. I wanted to receive the nutrients into my body, soul, and spirit that is my inheritance from my mountain.

As I spoke this request, I could see something like a heavenly substance being accessed from within the center of the mountain. The results of this are astonishing. At the end of July 2023, only two months later, God confirmed that I am receiving nutrients from my mountain through the testing that Dr. Robert Rodich does (see his website docrodich.com). Then my spirit said she would like more time to explore with me and show me places like my mountain. So instead of praying this time, just like Samuel answered to God's call in 1 Samuel 3, I said, "Here I am spirit!"

Again, I didn't realize it at the time, but this is more *heavenly alignment* and working together of my realms, as my spirit and body were now working together.

Then I saw greenery and a giant clover. I then realized it was a baby tree. I had learned that we have trees in the spirit, and I wanted the tree to grow, so I said, "I nurture the tree with my words, and I give it nutrients for the soil (from the Holy Spirit) and till the soil and then water it with living water (from the throne of God)." Then, I saw moss and envisioned myself taking off my shoes and walking in it. I didn't understand at the time that my spirit was showing me more of my inheritance, just like I asked. I have a new tree in the spirit that had started growing. Trees in the spirit represent, among other things: protection, governments, and believers growing in their sonship.

I didn't understand the moss part either at the time. Still, as I am reflecting, I understand because of what I learned from Dr. Robert Rodich at the Glory Conference that I went to in July with Dr. Ron Horner's ministry in North Carolina. Dr. Robert Rodich was the guest speaker there talking about our song and frequencies, and how Godly frequencies emanate from us. Putting my feet on the ground, on the moss around the base of the tree, also did something to nurture the tree because of my frequency and the song that emanates from me.

The anointing that comes from within us as sons of the Most High God, the Creator. We have been made in his image, and we have been given his ability. (Genesis 1:27 and John 14:12) Every place that the souls of our feet tread have been given to us

(Joshua 1:3). That encounter was profound, and the Lord was not finished.

Two weeks later, I was participating in a Zoom call with Dr. Ron Horner's ministry, and they were encouraging the Heavenly Alignment exercise. They impressed us with the importance of asking our realms to cooperate with each other daily. At that time, I was not doing it daily, just sporadically, although I did tell Ben about it and did it with him.

They shared testimonies and told us that if we were not aligning regularly, to ask our body, soul, and spirit what they needed to become comfortable with aligning our realms. I thought this was because they wanted to address the religious spirit that might be keeping people from doing it, but later, I realized it was because each of our parts: body, soul, and spirit have their own thoughts and emotions, and they may have things like grudges against each other—not being willing to work together. This comes from multiple things: our woundedness, trauma, and mostly our culture.

In our culture, we focus on our soul or body and completely leave our spirits out. We often don't acknowledge, mature, or grow in our spirit. This causes our soul to do all the work, so then our soul does not trust our spirit to do its job, because it hasn't for so long. It's not our spirit's fault.

We never acknowledged or engaged it or allowed it to operate. The same goes for our bodies. Some of us do not treat our bodies well. We do what the soul craves or our bodies crave, and it is harmful, unhealthy, or disrespectful to our bodies. Then, our bodies don't want to work with the soul.

It is important to ask each part of you what it needs to be comfortable cooperating with the other parts. The people sharing on the Zoom meeting shared that their souls felt overwhelmed and out of sorts, not knowing what was going on. So, Dr. Ron asked that the oil of ease be applied to their souls, and for their souls to be expanded to be able to handle these new revelations.

While they were working with the volunteers, I decided to do the exercise for myself. I asked my spirit how it was feeling, and then wrote down the first thoughts that came to my mind, understanding that those responses were from my spirit. My spirit said, "I am feeling excited about what you are learning and excited to share it and teach it to others."

I said, "Okay, you're fine."

Then, I asked my soul, "How are you feeling about this?"

My soul said, "I am concerned with how I will be received when my spirit shares this stuff with people." I recognized that as the fear of man, so I repented for fear of what people will think of me and for fear in general. I repented on behalf of myself and my bloodlines. Then I asked for the oil of ease for my soul and to be expanded. I felt better, more settled, like a sigh of relief.

Then, I asked my body, "How are you feeling about this?" I was a little concerned that I would not hear anything from my body because I still thought the first and only other time I tried to talk to my body, I didn't get anything that made sense. I apologized to my body for that.

First, I thought, "Full." I thought that made sense as I just finished lunch and was full. Then the next thought came to me, "Regretful."

I thought regretful, "Really?" Then, I started to analyze it. I thought, "Oh man, I shouldn't have eaten so much. I should have stopped when I was full and not finished my plate and overate."

Then the next thought came, "Regretful because I am not progressing like my spirit is. I feel like a failure." I thought, what!? "I feel like a failure!?"

Then I got sad that a part of me was feeling like a failure, and I realized it was true. My body had just come through being weak and unable to even do more than one chore a day at one point early the year before. I was making progress but still didn't feel like I was physically back up to the muscle strength and stamina that I had before the medical issue.

I didn't want any part of me to feel that way. I was sad that I felt like a failure, and I didn't even know it. I didn't know what to do about this, and panicked. My eyes were starting to tear, but since I was on the Zoom and they were helping people through the responses, I decided to raise my hand and share what was happening. As soon as I got to the part about my body, I started bawling my eyes out. They said it's okay. And that it was normal for emotions to come and be released. Then, they coached me by instructing me to tell my body out loud that everything will be okay and that my spirit will work with the Father, Son, and Holy Spirit to get my body up to par.

Then they instructed me to ask my body if that was okay. I felt it was fine with me, so I said, "Yes." Then, Dr. Ron continued to say that when we were taught to clean our plates, our bodies were being put into bondage. We were being taught not to listen to our bodies and not to practice self-control and problems for our bodies stem from that.

When we leave food on our plate, instead of cleaning our plates, we are practicing self-control. He repented on our behalf and on behalf of our parents and generations and the bad teachings that led them to instill these things in us. I thought it was very interesting because I didn't include all the internal thoughts I was having when I shared. Just that I was full, so I received that prayer and prayed along with it for the times I made my children finish their plates.

After that meeting, I felt relieved. I was reflecting on it, and it was as if some inner healing had just occurred. I knew the Lord was telling me, "Rachael, you need to engage each of the parts of your being and direct them to be in heavenly alignment every day, and you need to teach it to Ben." I was thinking, well, I did start teaching it to Ben. Then he said, "No, you need to teach him to do it on his own regularly, every day, then once he gets it down, he will no longer struggle with ADHD." I was shocked and in awe and said, "Yes, Lord, I will teach him." Ben was at day camp, so when he got home, I told him about it. He was excited, too! Then we did it the next morning before school. I learned about it through Dr. Ron's Tuesday night Mentorship meeting, but it is also in Dr. Robert Rodich's book *Moving Toward Sonship*.[12]

Immediately, there was confirmation that this was working. When Ben came home, I asked him if he felt it worked because he had taken the ADHD medication the day before at camp, and I wanted him to compare. He said it worked great, just *as if* he had taken the medication! I was rejoicing and jumping for joy!

Then, when my husband came home, Ben was sitting at the table eating chips, and he was not getting up and bouncing around the house and trying to eat chips on the fly. He was sitting quietly and still at the table eating his snack.

My husband asked me, "Of all the days to give Ben his medication, why did you decide to give it to him today when it's only him here and not a full house?" I smiled and got to tell him that I hadn't given him his medication and that we were trying a new therapy. He said, "Oh well, it works!"

It is amazing that God also had my husband confirm it. It works every single day, and we do it instantly. The enemy did try to discourage me, though as soon as my husband said that Ben started to act up again. I knew the enemy did not want my husband's agreement or backing that this works. I recognized it right away, and we did the Heavenly Alignment, asking our realms to cooperate with each other again, and it worked for the rest of the night.

---

[12] Available from docrodich.com.

Some days, we need to do it once in the morning and again later in the day, but *it always works!* It is also a struggle to get Ben to do it sometimes. He doesn't always want to. I know that is also the enemy, and I do tell him he has to do it, just like we would tell someone they need to take their medication even if they don't want to.

We think we should not force this kind of thing on our kids because it's a God thing, but God is showing me that is the wrong way to think. We must understand that we are the parents and have authority over our children while they are young. They do have choices to make, and they will make those choices when they get older and are on their own, but until then, our children's souls need to be in proper alignment.

When their souls align and work together with their spirit and body, then they will yield to the spirit and choose the things of God, of their design, and their destiny.

I had no recollection of the time we were following the prompting from Dr. Ron's *Commissioning Angels*[13] book, but now, looking back and reflecting on this journey to share it with you, I can see how the Lord was leading us to this. He was showing me what to do. I didn't get the full understanding then, but now I do.

---

[13] *Commissioning Angels – Volume 1* is available at www.RonHorner.com.

If we had asked for our spirit, soul, and body to work together daily instead of just that once, we would have seen similar progress. We needed it to be clearer, and the Lord clarified it for us and spelled out a process that covers us on all sides. Dr, Ron Horner and Dr. Robert Rodich are collaborating with the Most High God and each other and are continuing to refine this process as the Lord leads.

First, we started with aligning our realms: spirit, soul, and body, and directing them to cooperate with each other. This includes instruction to co-labor with the angels assigned to us and to operate from our destiny. The success was real, but the Lord was not finished; He continued speaking and teaching, and He still is. Following along with these amazing men of God, we then added our emotions which the Lord said are quantum and we added protection, resources, and inheritance to our daily routine of Heavenly Alignment.

At first, my soul said, "This is too long! This is too much to do every day." But I kept reminding myself that it is not. That is my soul still fearing that she has too much to do, listening to the fiery darts of the wicked one. I asked and sought God after this miracle, will I just throw it away due to impatience? Would I rather give my son's body a drug that we don't fully understand the ramifications of and roll the dice with an ungodly trade? Absolutely not! As for me and my family, we will follow God! I don't even need to wait for it to work! It works immediately!

It takes longer for medication to kick in than it does to do a Heavenly Alignment. The alignment does much more than just help with ADHD. It helps us in more ways than imaginable. This is a form of self-love. This is therapy. This is an answer to my prayers and seeking to understand mental illness and the relationship it has to the spiritual realm and how medication ties in. When should we take it, and when shouldn't we?

When we realize that aligning our realms is a means of loving ourselves. It helps us realize that our soul and our body are not our enemies. They are part of the equipping the Father has provided for each of us to experience wholeness.

Answers to my questions are becoming revealed through this process. The "...then once he gets it down, he will no longer struggle with ADHD" part says that this is an everyday thing that Ben needs to do right now, but it is not an everyday thing for the rest of his life. The 'how long' is unknown, but for now we know what to do.

The Lord then took this a step further and told me to apply it to someone close to me who was diagnosed with Bipolar Disorder and takes medication for it. The message was, "Don't stop taking your medication but get your being into alignment and your realms cooperating with each other regularly until it is again part of your nature. Continue to take the medication and do this as a prophetic act until you hear otherwise."

Chapter 12
Realm Angels and the Process

The Heavenly Alignment process is about acknowledging your body, speaking to it, and allowing it to be a part of your being that gives input. You are allowing it to provide you with information. Our bodies try to communicate with us, but we are not taught how to listen or communicate back. We are taught or programmed to ignore and reject our bodies. Think about it: what do we do? Do we listen to the pain? No. We ignore the pain (emotional and physical). But we are not designed to. We are designed to have pain (emotional and physical) so that the problem gets addressed. It's a trigger for us to recognize and reflect inward and to address the problem. Not to bury it, ignore it or project it outward and blame or put it on others.

Instantaneous healing does and can happen through the power and love of God, but God chooses to heal in many ways. We don't get to choose how God decides to heal a person. Many times, there is a journey, there is a process. God is orderly so we should accept the process. We should also not confuse the process by doing things the hard way at a lower level of the operation of godliness. We should also not confuse the process with human striving or trying to control or do things in our own power. Yes, we can get caught up in that if we are leaning on our own understanding and not continually in communication with God, we can end up doing things the hard way. We can end up circling the wilderness for 40 years like the Israelites until we start to listen, learn, and implement what the Lord is communicating to us.

The Lord is saying that this is a process. God has been showing me this through the way He has been speaking to me about Ben and his medicine—how following the process of Heavenly Alignment has been working. He has been showing me that we do the Heavenly Alignment every day and Ben doesn't need the medication to focus or sit still. He can focus! But, so far, the result doesn't linger into the following day. However, the Lord was speaking to me saying, "It's going to stay. His body needs to get used to that routine; it is a process."

The enemy is so against *processes* right now, even in the church, he is speaking to people that process is religion. We need to identify this lie.

> *I commission the angels to go capture those thoughts and to remove them, take them to the foot of the throne for judgment, to help us to make our thoughts obedient to us and the Lord and the Word of God and not just the written word but the living Word of God.*

We cannot come against the process. The process is our journey. Process is a huge part of our growth, and it is important. God is order, God is not chaos. Process is huge to God.

Lord, open the eyes of our understanding to this...to what you want to teach us about the process.

Part of what the Realm Angels do is to help us master the mind and take our thoughts captive. They are here to help us. As I shared before, I follow the "hearing God's voice" method or "protocol" and journal what the Ancient of Days, Father God, Jesus, Holy Spirit, my spirit, soul, body, and quantum emotions, say to me. I have come to the understanding that you can also talk to others in Heaven, the Men and Women in White, The Great Cloud of Witnesses, and even our Realm Angels in the same way.

A few days ago, I realized that I have not yet tried to listen for what my Realm Angels had to share with me. On September 23rd, I asked the question, "Realm Angels, what do you have to share with me today?"

They said, "Thank you for commissioning us, thank you for not leaving us out."

I said "You're welcome! Please help me to write about you well in my book(s)."

They said, "We are here to help." I thanked them again.

They said, "You need to understand who you are. You get to commission us. We want to help you. Commission us."

I asked, "Why does it seem like too much work, or too hard, or that it will take too much time to commission you, when I see the results when I do? And, the results are beyond anything I could have done myself or what would have happened according to the Laws of Logic or Big Physics!

They said "Your soul needs to be stretched in those moments. Do the stretching activity." (It's a prophetic act.)

I said, "Ok," and I stretched out my arms pulling my hands apart going front to back side to side, up and down, then diagonally, all the angles sometimes in an arch to try to encompass all of the stretching. Sometimes I also stretch out my legs in my chair or stand up and do it. As I stretch, I say, "I stretch my soul to become more... fill in the blank...." This time I said, "I stretch my soul to become more patient, willing, and diligent and to become a bigger vessel for God—a better landing place for Him and His glory and His love and His blessings and His work" Then I stretched some more and said, "I stretch my quantum emotions, spirit, and body also while I am at it." I invite you to do the stretching activity now.

Next, I asked, "Is zoning out or not focusing on the things around you and allowing your eyes to go out of focus considered "zoning out?" Is there a time and a place for it?" I was asking this because two days before, I was re-reading some teachings about Realm Angels. I read the April 18th blog post from ronhorner.com/blogs and the June 13th blog post on "Mastering the Mind." In the latter, it talks about escapism. To understand what the angels said to me, I think it is important for you to read the "Mastering the Mind" blog post updated June 15th.

Chapter 13
Mastering the Mind

By Dr. Ron Horner

[This chapter is from the blog post I just mentioned and is reprinted courtesy of Dr. Ron M. Horner of LifeSpring International Ministries, Inc. (RonHorner.com)]

Recently, Stephanie (Dr. Ron's Executive Assistant) and I were made aware of a different class of angels known as *Realm Angels*. These angels are assigned to each individual, and there are Realm Angels for one's soul, spirit, and body. They bring alignment and work dimensionally. One of their functions is to clean up the debris left in our lives from wrong relationships, and we have all had wrong relationships.

Their appearance is similar to Tinkerbell from the Disney movies; however they are not small like Tinkerbell but rather human-sized. Their wings may be effervescent in color.

They also can teach us about their roles, so our understanding is increased. As we engaged Heaven, one of Stephanie's Realm Angels appeared and began to teach us. We soon found ourselves in the Library of Revelation and were instructed to be seated.

The Realm Angel brought a book titled *Before the Foundations of the Earth* to the table. Stephanie turned the page and was transported to where the Father had conversed with each of her realms before the foundations of the earth. As the conversation ended, each realm stepped into the other of her realms, becoming one. Then, the Father began speaking to the Realm Angels as well. It was as if she was watching a bubble merge with another bubble like you would do with the child's liquid bubble toy. Each angel stepped into each bubble, and now, they were one. The Father took the one bubble, leaned over, and kissed it.

Suddenly, she was back in the room. Asking for an explanation of where she now was, the Realm Angel replied, "This is where you were originally constructed by the Father." Intuitively, Stephanie knew these Realm Angels had been with her since the beginning.

She began hearing the word 'escapism.' "What is that?" She asked.

Escapism

I replied, "Escapism is doing things to get your mind off what's going on around you. People do that with TV and movies."

The Realm Angel explained, "Escapism is powerless, mind-numbing, and futile. The instruction of the Lord to the Realm Angels is to bring people out of escapism." The Realm Angel asked, "Would you say the mind can be fragmented?"

"Yes," Stephanie replied.

The angel continued, "Is part of dimensional work gathering the bits and pieces of the fragmentations and going into different dimensions?"

Stephanie replied, "Yes, we're aware of that, but we have thought their souls are fragmented.

Realm Angel, "That is true, but these thoughts have been held captive. A person is unable to get past those thoughts. Our dimensional work brings back these thoughts of escapism."

Realm Angel instructed, "Read the text."

Stephanie remarked, "We know that spirit and soul can be fragmented and taken into different dimensions and realms, but what is the purpose of this understanding?

The Realm Angel replied, "It is our job to help minister to the fragments and bring them back. We can help master the mind."

Stephanie asked, "How so?"

The Realm Angel asked, "Can all things be explained?"

Stephanie remarked, "In the natural, I would say no."

Realm Angel asked, "Can all things be explained?"

Stephanie replied, "Can we explain all of fragmentation?"

Realm Angel further queried, "Where is truth?"

Stephanie said, "Truth is here in Heaven. Truth is Jesus and His Word."

The Realm Angel explained, "We are to bring back the truth. Can you "master the mind" if you have truth?"

Stephanie asked, "Isn't the mind the soul?"

The Realm Angel asked, "Is it?"

The angel explained, "Our job is to help master the mind. What are you instructed to take captive?"

Stephanie, "Our thoughts."

For though we walk in the flesh, we do not war according to the flesh. 4 For the weapons of our warfare are not carnal but mighty in God for pulling down strongholds, 5 casting down arguments and every high thing that exalts itself against the knowledge of God, bringing every thought into captivity to the obedience of Christ, 6 and being ready to punish all disobedience when your obedience is fulfilled. (2 Corinthians 10:3-6:)

The Realm Angel asked, "Would you say you've been good at that?"

Stephanie responded, "I have not been exceptionally good at that, no."

The angel asked, "What if you had help?"

Stephanie remarked, "Well, I have been taught that the Holy Spirit is our help in that."

The Realm Angel said, "We acknowledge that He is, but are there not more *for* you than against you?"

Stephanie asked, "How do you help us master the mind?"

Realm Angel asked, "Who is over the soul?"

Stephanie answered, "Jesus."

Realm Angel queried, "Is His Word not a calming effect on the mind?

Stephanie replied, "It is."

The Realm Angel asked, "If 'His word is a lamp into your feet and a light unto your path,' why have you not mastered the mind? If you have not mastered the mind, would you say everyone is fragmented to escapism?"

Stephanie asked, "Are you saying all?"

The Realm Angel instructed, "Turn the page."

As she did, the Realm Angel explained, "Our instruction is to bring the complete work of Jesus Christ to the mind, to the heart, to the unit that is the body. We do this dimensionally."

Stephanie asked, "How do we instruct you?"

The Realm Angel replied, "As you have been, to work dimensionally. Mastering the mind is not intellect; it is submission. Who can take the things captive and tear down the strongholds?"

Stephanie remarked, "You help us with that. don't you?"

The Realm Angel explained, "Per your instruction, we are a help in time of need."

Stephanie added, "I have a question about mastering the mind, because we are to live by the spirit."

The Realm Angel asked, "Is your mind not in full play?"

Stephanie replied, "Yes, it is."

Realm Angel commented, "Then master the mind. It is not in and of yourselves; it is the work of the Lord. We will help bring down strongholds; we are a very present help in time of need."

Stephanie explained, "I have a lot of questions. I just got a picture of how we have been numbing ourselves and our children at very early ages and teaching escapism instead of intimacy by sitting them in front of the TV."

I asked the Realm Angel, "So, what is the process?"

The Realm Angel remarked, "I thought you would never ask."

Stephanie, "I realize I have a huge religious spirit mindset around this. It's trying to cause and inflict fear. So, I lay that down. I'm willing to hear the truth."

What is adjudication?

The Realm Angel asked, "What is adjudication?"

I replied, "It is doing the court work necessary."

Turning to Stephanie, the Realm Angel asked, "What did you wake up on your mind with today?"

Stephanie replied, "The word I heard this morning was 'principled.' The definition of principled is acting according to morality and showing recognition of right and wrong based on a given set of rules.

"So, angel, in our processes of court work, is this where we present our mind to the Lord? What is this process? My mind keeps going back to the scripture, where we are to take our thoughts captive to the obedience of Christ. So, what is the best way to do that?

The Realm Angel instructed, "Commission us."

Stephanie described what she saw: "I see them helping us take captive our thoughts and the things that speak into our lives, spirit, and soul. They are helping to take these things captive. They are capturing, literally capturing things. Is that what we're to do?"

The Realm Angel replied, "We are your help in times of trouble."

Stephanie prayed,

> I ask the Father to forgive me for escapism. I have done it my entire life. I've taught my children to do it. And in the worldly sense, I have helped put them in captivity and put myself in captivity through escapism. I would like to be free from that, please. I repent, Father, and ask that you forgive me. I ask for the blood of Jesus to cover my sin and ask for the amendment of as if it never were.
>
> I request the angels to help master my mind around this and to take these thoughts captive that come, thoughts that are not of the Lord. I instruct you to do this in the mighty name of Jesus.
>
> Jesus, thank you. Father, thank you for putting these angels with me before the foundations of the world. I'm grateful that there's more for us than against us. And this is truly dimensional.
>
> Angel, I commission you to your work dimensionally around this, taking captive all these thoughts, and shutting the door in every dimension to escapism that I've opened.

The Realm Angel remarked, "How many have truly beat themselves up because they cannot control their thoughts?"

Stephanie added, "Well, that's true, but we have been doing court work for this a lot of times. Isn't that closing the door to generational sins?"

I asked, "How can we do it more effectively?"

The Realm Angel replied, "Close the door on escapism."

Stephanie governed,

> *In Jesus' name, I close every portal and every door that the enemy has used against my life and my dimensions. I close the door of escapism; however it was, and however it looked, over my entire life.*

The Realm Angel added, "Would you say that food is a form of escapism for many? Music is escapism. TV is escapism. Reading books full of pornography and the way of the world is escapism."

Stephanie responded, "It is."

The Realm Angel insisted, "Close the door to escapism."

Stephanie began a commission to the Realm Angel:

> *I commission you to close the door in all the dimensions as I have adjudicated to the Lord these sins that have been in my life. I bring my generations in and repent on behalf of my generations. We have all used escapism, a lie from the enemy. Forgive us, Lord.*

She added, "It's okay to watch TV. It's okay to chill, but being consumed with it is what the Realm Angel is talking about."

The Realm Angel replied, "There will be more. These are baby steps."

Stephanie remarked, "Well, we look forward to more training."

The angel then closed the book, put it back on the shelf and then came over and went inside Stephanie. As she did so, she said, "Master the mind. It's where you can truly have your thoughts taken captive quickly, efficiently, and effectively and not live in that bondage, but remember, you can't do it by yourself."

[End of blog post]

I did all the commissioning along with the blog post. As I said, I had been having trouble staying present at work the day after I read it. I knew I would add a chapter in this book about Realm Angels. In response to my question, "Is zoning out or not focusing on the things around you and allowing your eyes to go out of focus always considered escapism? Is there a time and a place for it?" The Realm Angels said, "No. You misinterpreted it." Immediately, I knew that was the religious spirit over me trying to confuse things. The Realm Angel said, "It is not always escapism in the sense that you should not always be present in the physical. When your focus is not on the things of this world, but on the things of Heaven, your focus is in another world, dimension, or realm. You don't need to fight it and try to stay present and focused in the physical when you intend to be present in the spiritual. We will help you to be present in the appropriate realm or dimension. We will help you not escape to a different realm or dimension or state of being or state of mind when you should be in the present or in the physical realm or vice versa. We will help you stay in the spiritual encounter and not get pulled out by physical distractions when you are in the spirit. We help you hone into what the Lord wants to speak to you or show you, so you don't miss it."

I said, "I always want to be in the spirit, be with and learn from God and do His work."

They said, "We know you do, but sometimes it is best to stay present in the physical. We will help you with that. We help you to take your thoughts captive and make them obedient to Christ."

I asked, "Why does my body sometimes want to go to sleep when I spend time in the spirit? Should I fight that and stay awake? I always thought that was the enemy trying to stop me from hearing or learning what God is teaching me."

Again, they said, "You misinterpret. Sometimes you are being moved or shifted to a new or different forum or experience."

I replied, "But I don't always remember the experience, hearing from God, or Heaven, or remember my dreams from that time."

They said, "That's OK. Your soul and body don't need to know or understand it all. Sometimes, your soul and body need to rest. They need to be recharged. Their schooling stops while your spirit's schooling continues."

Then it hit me. This is more help for Ben! This is more detail on how the Heavenly Alignment is helping him to be focused and not distracted in all different directions at once! We need to teach our children about the Realm Angels and how to commission them and how they help us. Our children need to master operating in unity and harmony with their whole being and in different dimensions and realms. They need to operate in this way even more than we do. We need the benefits, and we need to teach by example. This is also key to helping our kids *and* us when we are having nightmares. The Realm Angels help when we ask them to, to stay out of that dimension or realm that the enemy is trying to pull us into or keep us in when we are asleep. Don't take my word for it. Ask God to show you. Apply this, and you will see God's design at work for yourself.

Chapter 14
Aligning Your Realms Script

Since I have been speaking of Heavenly Alignment, I wanted to introduce you to a basic script I use to bring this about.

Aligning My Realms[14]

- **Spirit,** I acknowledge you and thank you for your role in my being.
- **Soul,** I acknowledge you and thank you for your role in my being.
- **Body,** I acknowledge you and thank you for your role in my being.
- **Quantum Emotional Realm.** I acknowledge you and thank you for your role in my being.

---

[14] Courtesy of Dr. Robert Rodich and Dr. Ron M. Horner.

- **Spirit,** I charge you to fulfill your role in unity and harmony with my soul and my body.
- **Soul,** I charge you to fulfill your role in unity and harmony with my spirit and body.
- **Body,** I charge you to fulfill your role in unity and harmony with my spirit and soul.
- **Quantum Emotional Realm,** I charge you to fulfill your role in unity and harmony with my spirit, soul, and body.

- **Father,** I invite you to have dominion over my spirit, and I yield dominion to you this day.
- **Jesus,** I invite you to have dominion over my soul, and I yield dominion to you this day.
- **Holy Spirit,** I invite you to have dominion over my body, and I yield dominion to you this day.
- **Ancient of Days,** I invite you to have dominion over my quantum emotional realm, and I yield dominion to you this day.

- I commission all my realms to work in tandem with **Father, Son, Holy Spirit, and Quantum Emotional Realm.**

- I charge the angels over my realms to work with all the angels assigned to me today.
- I charge the angels assigned to me to work with the Bond Registry Angels, as well as the angels over my realms.

- I charge all the angels of my realms, and my personal angels to diligently labor for the fulfillment of my scroll.
- I bless these angels in their work with Angel Elixir, Angel Food, Angel Bread, and other such things as they need for the fulfillment of their assignments.
- I bless my spirit, soul, and body, and instruct my soul and body to yield to my spirit this day.

I thank you all for the good job that you do.

Chapter 15
The Ancient of Days

I was sharing with a friend and said, "The Holy Spirit is all over me when I address the Ancient of Days." I am not saying it's like a fourth part of the Trinity, but I know that the Ancient of Days wants us to communicate with Him the way we communicate with the Father, Son, and Holy Spirit.

I see The Ancient of Days as the whole encompassed Spirit of the Lord, the Godhead all together. The Lord told me the Ancient of Days is the Godhead in the quantum emotional realm. Our emotions were defiled and separated from God at the fall, and they were turned inward towards ourselves and into selfishness. The fall made our emotions about ourselves, when God's emotions are supposed to be driving us. We are to be allowing His emotions to flow out of us, and that is to drive us to do His work in love for people.

What the Lord is saying is that the Ancient of Days rules over the quantum emotional realm in an undefiled state and when we align ourselves with the Heavenly Alignment process, we align ourselves with *and in* relationship with God. Then, we can access restored emotions and a restored soul and body. That is what Jesus did on the cross.

We are in alignment when we are restored and operating with a renewed mind. It's the state we were in before Adam's fall, and we can operate that way because of what Jesus did on the cross.

The old man has passed away, and there is a new man. We have a new nature. Our old nature is gone. We don't have to wait. We are who He created us to be now. We can operate that way, but we must know that we can. We need to understand and walk in it. That's what this whole sonship journey is. We need to stop thinking we cannot.

The same with our bodies. Every time I hear someone talking about our bodies and how they are decaying and how they are in a fallen state, not going to be restored until Jesus returns, I don't agree.

> *But we are citizens of Heaven, where the Lord Jesus Christ lives. And we are eagerly waiting for him to return as our Savior. He will take our weak mortal bodies and change them into glorious bodies like his own, using the same power with which he will bring everything under his control. (Philippians 3:20-21) (NIV)*

I pray and bless God's people on our body journeys to come to know and understand and respect our bodies and understand that our bodies are also restored. Our bodies are degenerating or going in the opposite direction of life because of agreements that we, or our ancestors, made with the enemy somewhere along the line. It's not how we should be.

Once we are renewed, once Jesus died on the cross, we don't need to die anymore. But we don't get it, and we put all these word curses on ourselves, standing in unbelief, in disbelief. Once we get to the bottom of what the enemy has on us, we stop believing his lies, and we start to understand our legal rights and where he thinks he has legal rights. Once we remove those strongholds he is standing on or impressing against us, once we come into the full understanding of what Jesus's sacrifice on the cross did for us, who we are in Christ and with Christ in us, then our body will come into alignment, and we will not suffer anymore. We also will not hunger. We will live via the provision of the spirit. We are already whole and restored, but when we don't know it, it allows the enemy to steal from us. The understanding and knowledge that we no longer stand in decaying bodies will move our bodies in the process of our bodies being renewed and restored.

I bless my body; I bless your body; I bless our children's bodies to come into alignment—come into the blessing of the sacrifice of what Jesus did for our bodies. I believe this. I didn't always believe this, but I do now. I needed to speak it out and birth it into fruition for my understanding and for my body, for myself, and for my family so I could teach it to my children and put it into this book.

Chapter 16
A New Master Blueprint

We are in a process of restoration, restoring us to our original design before the fall of man when Adam and Eve sinned in the Garden of Eden. This doesn't just apply to those who struggle with physical illness or mental illness.

We have a blueprint[15] or template that our being works from. That is how our quantum parts know how to be arranged, stay together, and work together. Science helps us to understand this in the physical realm. There are keys in physics and quantum physics, but we don't need to know all the intricate details. That is supplemental and fun for some of us to learn about. The connection to the spiritual realm is much more important, and we must start teaching it to our children. Imperfections get into our blueprints through sin, missing the mark, which grows into a transgression and is repeated, that

---

[15] The book *Building Your Business with the Blueprint of Heaven* by Dr. Ron M. Horner is available from www.RonHorner.com.

then gets twisted into an iniquity, saying that wrong is right and operating as if it is right, okay, normal, and natural yet it goes against nature and the principles of God. This leads to changes in our blueprints that need to be restored to the original design. I was first introduced to blueprints when Dr. Ron Horner's ministry started discussing it in their Tuesday night mentorship meetings. Then Jeremy Friedman, who works with Dr. Ron as part of the Heaven Down Business team, began talking about them in relationship to running businesses.

Next, my pastor David Daminani mentioned them during our church service, and my spirit jumped for joy! Then, Dr. Robert Rodich shared about them in the mentorship meeting with Dr. Horner and again in July at the Glory conference. Repetition is one of the ways God speaks to us. Nothing is a coincidence. When things are being brought up multiple times, I know to pay attention, and the Lord is saying something.

At first, I thought blueprints were the same thing as our scroll, which is what the Father has written about us before we were born (Hebrews 10:7, Psalm 40:7). But now I understand it is more about the design. It is the layout of our beings, not what we do or are to do. Our blueprint is not our destiny or purpose.

Why am I talking about blueprints? I want you to know about them so you can understand that in the fall, our design shifted, and our blueprint changed. So, how we are configured now is different from the way we were originally intended to be.

I learned from Dr. Robert Rodich that we can ask Heaven for a new heavenly blueprint for something like a new cardiovascular system or a new heart. Then, we ask God to insert his creative light and blessing into it. Then we, filled with the Holy Spirit, can fix ourselves, our anointing with the different portions of the Holy Spirit, which each cover the frequencies of the color spectrum.

Once it is combined, we can release it onto the heavenly blueprint and receive it into our soul. This makes it a multi-dimensional blueprint. Once multi-dimensional, the blueprint is prepared to manifest in the physical. Our soul is the portal where the new heavenly blueprint is brought into this reality from the spiritual realm.

From our soul, we release it (via our words) to whoever or whatever the blueprint is meant for and watch as it manifests and miracles happen. I made requests for my family members and their body systems.

Then, Dr. Robert Rodich had this idea to request a new Master Blueprint for our entire being. So, let's request that for our children. Speak out loud:

> We request from Heaven a new Master blueprint for our own and our children's Quantum emotions, a new Master Blueprint for our own and our children's Spirit, a new Master Blueprint for our own and our children's soul, a new Master Blueprint for our own and our children's body.
>
> We now ask the Ancient of Days to insert his creative light and blessing into these Master Blueprints that we have requested.
>
> We repent for any ungodliness within us and our children, and we ask the Holy Spirit to fill us.

We mix all portions of ourselves, our light, and our anointing with the portions of the Holy Spirit and the Holy Spirit's light, each color of the spectrum and release it into these new Master Blueprints.

We thank you for intermingling and combining, and now we release each of them onto our souls.

We receive the blueprints into our soul to become a multi-dimensional Master blueprint, and we release each Master Blueprint to its proper portion of our being and our children's beings in Jesus' name and by the power of His blood, the Holy Spirit, and the Ancient of Days fire within us.

We ask for the fire of the Ancient of Days to come and burn up any membranes or restrainers holding our beings out of place and out of order in Jesus' Mighty name.

Chapter 17
Prophetic Acts and More Revelation

As mentioned, the Lord has been speaking to me about the importance of prophetic acts. He started by using Ben and how he is constantly acting out what he is doing in the spirit with his movement and motion. He continued this conversation with me after doing the frequency print with Dr. Robert Rodich.

Dr. Rodich does testing that measures energy and frequency. Through the readouts, he can tell about physical things such as what nutrients we are missing, which muscles or organs are not functioning properly, or if we have an imbalance of something, even if we have a parasite in our system.

He can also tell about spiritual things like where our body is holding on to trauma, what kind of spiritual attack we are under, what area of emotional healing is needed, and how we commune with God. My readout told the story of an imbalance of parasites in my body; however, the nutrient deficiencies did not match up with the ramifications of having parasites. When things do not add up physically, it is an indication that something spiritual is going on. This was the confirmation that I had received the nutrients my body needed through access to my spiritual inheritance, my spiritual mountain.

On August 2nd, 2023, during my morning time with God, He told me about a shift and that I was changed that day. He said, "You are deep, you are loved." Since I was hearing so clearly from Him, I decided to ask about the diatomaceous earth that Dr. Rodich prescribed me to take care of the parasites. When I received the news that I had parasites, I went to prayer and asked for the fire of the Ancient of Days to burn up the parasites. I believed that they were gone, but I continued to take the diatomaceous earth.

I was trying to decide or understand if I should continue in the physical to take it. I felt that I should continue, and I didn't stop taking it, but I asked, "Why, Lord, do you want me to keep taking the diatomaceous earth if I believe you healed me?" His Answer was, "It's a prophetic act of faith. It's similar to a person taking medicine with the power of witchcraft behind it. They have faith that they are going to achieve their goal. It's a prophetic act backed by faith. It's a ritual. You believe that when someone who is practicing witchcraft sets out to accomplish something with their mixing of things and rituals, they will be successful, don't you?"

I answered, "Yes, Lord, I believe that stuff is real, and there is power behind it from the evil one that will manifest."

Then the Lord said, "How much more should you do my prophetic acts? Why wouldn't you follow through with prophetic acts for the Kingdom of God instructed by God? The man of God told you to take the diatomaceous earth, so you take it exactly as you were told. Not more, not less." My immediate response was, "Okay, I will keep on doing it! I repent for not recognizing your prophetic acts and questioning following through with them. I didn't understand, but now that you are telling me this is a prophetic act, I will not question it; I will do it."

Our children are just like this. They need patience and explanation, forgiveness, and mercy. I recognized at this moment that the Lord was helping me to overcome the religious spirit, the enemy's lies that were telling me in my subconscious, "If you continue taking diatomaceous earth, then you are not believing your miracle will happen." Which is exactly what the enemy was trying to do! He was trying to stop me from obtaining the miracle, by not following through with the prophetic act!

I thanked God for this revelation and for taking the veils off my eyes and mind. Just then, Ben started calling out to me from his room, and I could tell from the way he was calling and not responding to my answer that he was being attacked with some kind of nightmare; something was not right.

When I got to his room, he was sitting up in bed and trying to rub his back. He said he got attacked in the back by a giant bee in his sleep. This hurt my heart because I knew it was a spiritual attack. Last summer, Ben got stung in the lip by a hornet, and he had a full body reaction—a rash, hives, and his entire face swelled up. It was a slow, gradual reaction, but by the time I got him to urgent care, you couldn't recognize him; he looked like a completely different person.

Since then, we have been carrying an EpiPen with us even though we brought it to the Courts of Heaven and received a new heavenly verdict about Ben and allergies and are declaring and standing on the verdict that he is healed, and he is not going down this path of escalating reactions to bee stings. I also have peace about it when we do forget to bring the EpiPen somewhere. I could see that this was an attack of fear on him. I immediately reminded him, "What is the first thing you do? You use your scripture weapon and speak it out loud. I do not have a spirit of fear. I have a spirit of power, and of love, and of a sound mind." (2 Timothy 1:7) Then the Lord said, "Apply what I just told you about prophetic acts to the EpiPen." I said silently to the Lord, "Okay, Lord, it doesn't translate in my mind like this, but I will do my best because you told me to. Let the words flow from my mouth." So, I said to Ben, "We don't carry around the EpiPen out of fear that you are going to react because we know that you are healed. We carry it with us as a prophetic act of obedience because Godly council told us to. So, we continue until we hear otherwise from the Lord.

"It is not because we don't believe that you are healed. We keep it until God specifically says stop carrying it around."

Ben accepted this, laid back down, snuggled up and went back to sleep. It was still early morning. As I returned to my room to finish my morning with God, He said, "Now apply this to your friend and tell your friend this." I was speechless. I had shared Ben's Heavenly Alignment testimony with my friend a week or two before and how it applied to him and bipolar struggles.

I told him to acknowledge each part of his being, align his realms, give God dominion over each part, and gave him the example to follow. I was sure to emphasize that what God told us was that this was not an immediate thing; it is a process.

Ben needs to get in the habit of doing the Heavenly Alignment on his own, regularly, meaning every day. Then, once he gets it down, and not before, he will no longer struggle with ADHD.

So, I told my friend, "The same goes for you; don't stop taking your medication to do the Heavenly Alignment; do both." I didn't share it with him a few months prior when God was initially speaking to me about Ben because I wanted to be sure I had all the information first and that God was confirming that this is not just for Ben and applies elsewhere.

I wanted to make sure it would not be interpreted or received wrong, twisted, or misconstrued. I wanted God's blessing to share it so the enemy could not take it and run with it and cause problems. There is a responsibility that comes along with the words that we speak.

I shared with my friend a few weeks after God said, "Share this with your friend." Wait for God's nudging and prompting. Sometimes, He is blatantly clear. He wasn't always.

At first, it was a nudge/hunch, but the more I listen and follow through with the nudges, the closer I get to Him in my walk and the clearer I hear Him. Walking down the hall this time, He said very clearly, "Now apply it to your friend." I was celebrating and rejoicing, and my spirit was saying, "Fire of Ancient of Days! Fire of Ancient of Days!"

Then I saw a vision, a stick with jewelry on it. Like a beaded bracelet and realized it was a scepter! I received a scepter from God! And he said, "You shall live and not die!"

I called my friend and shared with him what had just gone down. I told him about the prophetic act of taking diatomaceous earth, using the EpiPen, and taking bipolar medication. I said, "You're not continuing to take the bipolar medication out of fear that you are going to be dependent on it for the rest of your life because we know that you are healed. You must take it as a prophetic act of obedience because Godly council told you to. Continue to follow the prescription from the Godly counsel until you hear otherwise from the Lord. It is not because we don't believe that you are healed or that it will work. We continue to do the prophetic act until God specifically says stop taking the medication."

On August 7th, 2023, God was still talking to me about prophetic acts. The Lord said to exercise. We need to exercise our legs like the man at church needed to walk around the sanctuary."

I asked God, "Was that your idea?" because I prayed for the man. My hands were tingling with the power of God the Sunday before at church, so I asked if anyone wanted prayer for healing. After service a man in a wheelchair was brought up, and I, along with others in the church, prayed for him. I felt the power in my hands, and after I put them on the man, it went out of my hands.

So, I told him to stand up out of the wheelchair. I thought it was a prophetic act. And stand he did.

Then I heard the Lord say, "Walk it out, walk it out." So, I told him, "Walk it out, walk it out," and he did. But he didn't run. He sat back down in the wheelchair after making it around the sanctuary. The Lord knew I had questions about why he sat back down.

When I asked, "Was that your idea?" God said, "What did I tell you the other day? Speak it. Speak your ideas as though they are mine because they are. I put the ideas there in your heart—confidence, boldness. Confidence and Boldness."

Then I saw the tail of an airplane, and He said, "You are going somewhere, Rachael. You saw it. You envisioned that man moving faster and faster, running, jumping, and dancing. I wanted him to; he could have. It's not too late. Once you are in a realm in Heaven while still on Earth, once you experience an experience, you can always get back there. Tell them. Tell them. Tell Benny."

I decided I needed to stretch because I must have been feeling overwhelmed. So, I prophetically stretched my arms out in every direction, saying, "I stretch my quantum spirit; I stretch my quantum soul. I stretch my quantum body; I stretch my quantum emotions so that I can handle and experience the things God has in all directions.

Then I saw a big space, a big container. I felt at peace, I felt ok, like what God just said was completely obtainable. I knew it was from within that was expanded, but even the room I was in, in the physical, looked bigger and felt more spacious.

Then he said, "Stretch and expand with Benny regularly. That will also help with the eye rolling and attitude. When he does that, his soul needs stretched and expanded and so does yours. I am meeting you. I am meeting all your needs. I am healing you; I am restoring you, even the little stuff, toenails, the bump in the right palm of your hand. We will add stretching and expanding with prophetic acts to our daily Heavenly Alignment commissioning. I highly recommend you add it to you and your children's day as well. You can find it in Chapter 11.

Two days later, during my morning devotions, the Lord said, "I have good gifts for you. I have promises for you. Go through your vision list and add to it. Do more Freedom from Freemasonry court work and the associated victory declarations." Then he gave me notes for this parenting book, and I wrote the steps just like that, a download from Heaven on what to say. And the rest is history.

Chapter 18
Review

In this book, we have learned several different methods of spiritual warfare:

1. The first one is praying out loud. Our ears need to hear our interaction with Heaven.
2. Read scripture aloud and do a word search. Our words build in the spirit when we read scripture out loud.
3. Paraphrase Bible stories and speak out the lessons, encouragement, and prophecy that comes from them. Speak out the rest of the story as it is in the Word, and prophesy over your situation so that it will manifest over you physically.
4. Claim the promises of God.
5. **Use imagination as a machine to build things in the spirit that aid us in victory** (See it. Think it. Speak it. Believe it.) Our soul helps to bring it to fruition on earth.

6. **Petition your requests in court case format** going after the legal ground in the Courts of Heaven.
7. **Inner Healing**, revisit where parts of you are stuck, and work through them with Jesus. As you do, the enemy's plans for you are smashed, and you see changes in the physical.

Appendix

Opening Prayer[16]

Whenever I am going to conduct a ministry session, I will always say a prayer to open the session. Opening in prayer sets the atmosphere and establishes ground rules in the spirit. There are many ways to open a ministry session in prayer. Below is a sample prayer that includes some of the key points I like to cover before beginning to minister to an individual or a group.

> *Father God, we come before you in the mighty name of Jesus Christ. We praise you for this day, as it is the day that you have made, and we will rejoice and be glad in it.*

---

[16] Duval, Daniel. *Prayers That Shake Heaven and Earth* (p. 55). Covenant House Publishing LLC. Kindle Edition.

We enter your gates with thanksgiving and into your courts with praise. We assume the armor of God: The helmet of salvation, the breastplate of righteousness, the belt of truth, our feet are shod with the preparation of the gospel of peace, we take up the shield of faith that quenches every fiery dart of the wicked one, and the sword of the Spirit, which is the word of God, praying with all prayer and supplication in the Spirit. We also take up the garments of vengeance and the cloak of zeal. We declare that where two or three are gathered in your name, you are in our midst.

Lord Jesus, you stand at the door and knock, and to him who opens it for you, you will come in and you will sup with him. We open the door to you and invite you to establish your presence in our midst.

We declare right now that every amnesic wall, barrier, blockade, stronghold, or veil that would otherwise hinder progress and get in the way is put to sleep, disengaged, and moved out of the way in Jesus' name. Every curse, hex, vex, spell, incantation, form of witchcraft, voodoo, dark art, or other form of weaponized demonic activity are reversed upon the heads of the senders seven-fold that they would know that Jesus is Lord.

We declare that every human spirit, hybrid spirit, demonic spirit, synthetic spirit, or spirit child on assignment to create distraction, confusion, or the triggering of bombs, tripwires, booby traps, or other types of programming are now discovered, bound in chains and fetters of iron, and put wherever the True Lord Jesus sends them.

We thank you, Holy Spirit of Truth, that you are present to lead us and guide us into all truth, for you do not speak of yourself, but whatever you hear, that you speak, and you show us things to come.

We call this session very fruitful, and we thank you in advance, Lord Jesus, for the healing and breakthrough that will manifest during this time. Amen.

Closing Prayer[17]

My prayer books are used by people all over the world, not just for personal work but in the context of pastoral counseling, life coaching, clinical psychology (with consenting clients), and deliverance work. As such, it has been pointed out on many occasions that I have an Opening Prayer, but not a Closing Prayer. This has been a major point of confusion and, as such, has caused many people to ask the same question, "Did I miss something?" I have had many people ask me the question, "How do you conclude a session?"

To be completely honest, when I am working with people, I have found that ensuring they are feeling stable and emotionally settled is much more important than ensuring I get a prayer template spoken over a person that is feeling frazzled, rattled, or steamrolled. No one enjoys a practitioner that leaves them feeling like chop suey at the end of their session. Nonetheless, I

---

[17] Duval, Daniel. *Extreme Prayers that Shake Heaven and Earth* (p. 52). Covenant House Publishing LLC. Kindle Edition.

am providing a basic closing prayer template here for those that have been bothered by the fact that I did not provide a closing prayer template before. This is not the be-all and end-all of closing prayers, but it is short and easily deployable, and should be used at the conclusion of bringing a client, friend, or parishioner to a place of emotional and psychological stability at the end of a counseling, coaching, or deliverance session. This prayer is a short statement that will tie up some loose ends at the conclusion of a session and allow for the dismissal of avoidable backlash for the person receiving ministry. This template can and should be expanded and tailored as appropriate by the practitioner but provides some strong foundational bones and will do a great job as written. Enjoy!

> *Father God, we come before you in the mighty name of Jesus Christ. I thank you for the fruit of this session and I speak that it will be fruit that remains. I thank you, Jesus Christ, that you are our Shield, Buckler, Rearguard, Strong Tower, and Fortress. I speak that we leave this session by entering into your protection and under the shadow of your wings.*
>
> *I call for the interruption of evil agendas designed to bring backlash. Specifically, I place angels on assignment to watch over doors that have been closed, and to arrest and lock down all evil, confused, fearful, cult loyal, or well-meaning yet deceived alters, parts, splinters, shards, fragments, RNA, DNA, and frequencies that would reopen doors to enemy agents subsequent to this session. I declare that astral reporters will be intercepted in all attempts to report to handlers, programmers, or agents of evil, and escorted into the immediate presence of the True Lord Jesus*

Christ, in addition to all of their backups. I speak that we are protected by heavenly equations and force fields, ensuring that evil assaults are interrupted before they are noticed. I booby-trap evil assignments taken out against us with spiritual weapons of mass destruction, bringing severe pain and ruin to agents of darkness engaging in evil assignments against us after this session. We also sever and release any ungodly transfers or entanglements between us that may have occurred during the execution of this session.

Furthermore, I thank you, Lord God, that you give us the peace which passes all understanding that will keep our hearts and minds by Christ Jesus. I thank you for your faithfulness to finish the good work that you have begun in us, in Jesus's name. Amen.

The Names of God

El Emunah	(Deut. 7:9)	The Faithful God
El Hakabodh	(Ps. 29:3)	The God of Glory
El Hay	(Josh. 3:10)	The Living God
El Kanna	(Ex. 20:5)	Jealous God
El Nekamoth	(Ps. 18:47)	God that Avenges
El Nose	(Ps. 99:8)	God who Forgave
El Rai	(Gen. 16:13)	God that Sees Me
El Simchath Gili	(Ps. 43:4)	God my Exceeding Joy
El-Elyon	(Gen. 14:18)	The Most-High God
Elohe Chaseddi	(Ps. 59:10)	The God of my Mercy
Elohe Tishuathi	(Ps. 18:46)	God of my Salvation
Elohe Yisrael	(Ps. 59:5)	God of Israel

Elohenu Olam	(Ps. 48:14)	Our Everlasting God
Elohim Kedoshim	(Josh. 24:19)	Holy God
Elohim Ozer Li	(Ps. 54:4)	God My Helper
El-Olam	(Gen. 21:22)	The Everlasting God
El-Roy	(Ps. 23:1)	The Lord my Shepherd
El-Shaddai	(Gen. 17:1,2)	God Almighty
Jehovah Adon Kol Ha-arets	(Josh 3:11)	The Lord of All the Earth
Jehovah El Emeth	(Ps. 31:5)	Lord God of Truth
Jehovah Elohe Yisrael	(Ps. 41:13)	The Lord God of Israel
Jehovah Goelekh	(Isa. 49:26)	The Lord our Redeemer
Jehovah Immeka	(Judges 6:12)	The Lord is with You
Jehovah Izuz Wegibbor	(Ps. 24:8)	The Lord Strong and Mighty
Jehovah Machsi	(Ps. 91:9)	The Lord my Refuge
Jehovah Magen	(Deut. 33:29)	The Lord the Shield
Jehovah Maginnenu	(Ps. 89:18)	The Lord Our Defense
Jehovah Mauzzi	(Jer. 16:19)	The Lord my Fortress
Jehovah Melech Olam	(Ps. 10:16)	The Lord King Forever

Jehovah Mephalti	(Ps. 18:2)	The Lord My Deliverer
Jehovah Metsudhathi	(Ps. 18:2)	The Lord my High Tower
Jehovah Moshiekh	(Isa. 49:26)	The Lord our Savior
Jehovah Ori	(Ps. 27:1)	The Lord my Light
Jehovah Roi	(Ps, 23:1)	The Lord my Shepherd
Jehovah Sali	(Ps, 18:2)	The Lord my Rock
Jehovah-Elohim	(Isa. 43:10-11)	The Lord God Creator
Jehovah-Gibbor	(Heb. 11:3)	The Lord Almighty
Jehovah-Hoseenu	(Ps. 95:6-7)	The Lord of Recompense
Jehovah-Jireh	(Gen. 22:14)	The Lord Our Provider
Jehovah-Makeddesh	(Lev. 20:8)	The Lord Who Sanctifies
Jehovah-Nissi	(Ex. 17:13-16)	The Lord Our Banner
Jehovah-Rapha	(Luke 5:20)	The Lord Our Healer
Jehovah-Sabbaoth	(1 Sam. 1:3)	The Lord of Hosts
Jehovah-Shalom	(John 14:6-7)	The Lord of Peace
Jehovah-Shammah	(Ezek. 48:35)	The Lord Who is Present/There
Jehovah-Tsidkenu	(Jer. 33:14-18)	The Lord Our Righteousness

Jehovah-Tsuri	(Ps. 18:2)	The Lord Our Strength
Yeshuah Ha Mashiach		Jesus the Messiah

Ministries Mentioned

In this book I have mentioned several ministries that have been instrumental in my journey. Their basic information is listed here for your convenience.

Daily Audio Bible	DailyAudioBible.com
Arthur Burk	TheSLG.com
Dr. Robert Rodich	DocRodich.com
Daniel Duval	BrideMovement.com
Dr. Ron M. Horner	RonHorner.com
Jeremy Friedman	LighthouseFM.net

About the Author

Rachael is a working mom with a blended family. Her passion is seeing her children maximize their potential and become spiritual giants. As a believer in Jesus who grew up in church, her relationship has really deepened over the past several years. The deepening started when she stopped passing up opportunities to speak about God and Jesus (saying no to the Holy Spirit), and when she started to engage her spirit. Rachael seeks to know the Father more and more intimately and see the promises of God fulfilled in not only her life but those of her family, friends and others.

Description

Rachael Testa's *Engaging Your Imagination for Raising Godly Children: How to Create Spiritual Giants* is an encouraging book for parents seeking to nurture a child's spiritual growth through the power of the imagination as well as acknowledging and engaging their spirit.

From the foundational role of exposing your child to scripture to the profound impact of worship and spoken prayers, each chapter is a treasure trove of insights and actionable guidance.

The book also transcends conventional techniques, connecting the spirit realm and imagination and delving into practices like speaking spirit to spirit and aligning your realms. Visualization as a faith technique is discussed to access the Kingdom realm of Heaven.

Engaging Your Imagination for Raising Godly Children is not just a guidebook; Testa provides a holistic resource for cultivating a child's spiritual journey and invites you on a profound exploration of faith with her children, equipping you with the tools and wisdom to guide the next generation toward a deeply rooted and vibrant spiritual life.

Published by:

A Division of LifeSpring Publishing
www.scrollpublishers.com

Has God spoken to you about writing a book? Let us help you!

www.ingramcontent.com/pod-product-compliance
Lightning Source LLC
Chambersburg PA
CBHW031631160426
43196CB00006B/368